1456

The media's watching Vault! Here's a sampling of our coverage.

"For those hoping to climb the ladder of success, [Vault's] insights are priceless."
– Money magazine

"The best place on the web to prepare for a job search."
– Fortune

"[Vault guides] make for excellent starting points for job hunters and should be purchased by academic libraries for their career sections [and] university career centers."
– Library Journal

"The granddaddy of worker sites."
– US News and World Report

"A killer app."
– New York Times

One of Forbes' 33 "Favorite Sites"
– Forbes

"To get the unvarnished scoop, check out Vault."
– Smart Money Magazine

"Vault has a wealth of information about major employers and job-searching strategies as well as comments from workers about their experiences at specific companies."
– The Washington Post

"A key reference for those who want to know what it takes to get hired by a law firm and what to expect once they get there."
– New York Law Journal

"Vault [provides] the skinny on working conditions at all kinds of companies from current and former employees."
– USA Today

VAULT GUIDE TO RESUMES, COVER LETTERS & INTERVIEWS

VAULT GUIDE TO RESUMES, COVER LETTERS & INTERVIEWS

HOWARD LEIFMAN, PhD, MARCY LERNER
AND THE STAFF OF VAULT

NEW AGE INTERNATIONAL PUBLISHERS
2006

Printed in India at Saras Graphics, Delhi
1 2 3 4 5 6 7 8 9 10

ISBN: 81-224-1703-5
Original Edition Price: $19.95
Indian Edition: Rs.145/-
C-05-06-167

PUBLISHING FOR ONE WORLD
NEW AGE INTERNATIONAL (P) LIMITED, PUBLISHERS
(formerly Wiley Eastern Ltd.)
New Delhi • Bangalore • Chennai • Cochin • Guwahati • Hyderabad
Jalandhar • Kolkata • Lucknow • Mumbai • Ranchi
Visit us at **www.newagepublishers.com**

Acknowledgments

Vault would like to take the time to acknowledge the assistance and support of Matt Doull, Ahmad Al-Khaled, Lee Black, Eric Ober, Hollinger Capital, Tekbanc, New York City Investment Fund, American Lawyer Media, Globix, Ingram, Hoover's, Glenn Fischer, Mark Hernandez, Ravi Mhatre, Tom Phillips, Carter Weiss, Ken Cron, Ed Somekh, Isidore Mayrock, Zahi Khouri, Sana Sabbagh, Esther Dyson and other Vault investors, as well as our loving families and friends.

Thanks also to Marcy Lerner and Kelly Shore.

Table of Contents

Table of Contents

Introduction

It's time for you to look for a job. Maybe it's your first job, maybe it's a job in a new field, or maybe it's just an improvement over the slave pit in which you now toil. Whatever the reason, Vault, Inc., the workplace network, knows how to get you hired. We've talked to hiring managers, human resources officers, executives and employees involved in the hiring process from every major career field. From that wealth of information and expertise, we've compiled a guide with the power to get you on the payroll.

Wondering how we'll do it? Here's how.

One book sitting on the career guides shelf might offer advice on how to ace an interview, while another might offer tips on writing an attention-grabbing cover letter. A third might tell you how to put together a succinct resume. But because these books artificially separate the key elements of the employment process, job seekers end up unevenly prepared, and fail to see the process through to its completion.

That's why the *Vault Guide to Resumes, Cover Letters & Interviews* is unique: it offers a complete approach to the art of landing a job, a complete arsenal with which the reader can challenge — and crush — the competition. This guide will enable you to perfect every aspect of your job hunting technique.

RESUMES

Overview

"This will be good for my resume." That's the mantra of the young and upwardly mobile, muttered at the threshold of every unpleasant task. But what does the phrase really mean? What exactly goes into resumes, anyway? What gets left out? And why do resumes even matter? If you're asking yourself these things, you're far from alone.

Your resume: your career history, your years of education, your commitment to your employers, your dreams all ascribed on a sheet of white or ecru paper titled, at the top, with your name. (Or perhaps, e-mailed to employers far and wide.) But to be effective, a resume must adhere to one rule: Information must be delivered in an attractive, efficient, and easily accessible manner.

The properly prepared resume of a less experienced candidate can trump a poor resume from a more experienced candidate. The difference between a good resume and a bad one is the difference between a new job and continued unemployment. But armed with the proper instruction on how to negotiate the art, writing a powerful, clear resume can be as easy as filling out a form.

Here's how.

Your Life on a Page

CHAPTER 1

THINK YOU'RE INEXPERIENCED AT WRITING RESUMES? YOU MAY NOT BE QUITE AS BAD AS YOU THINK. READ ON FOR A CAUTIONARY EXAMPLE.

Myron Hardy

440 Carlotta Towers
Minton University
Ebbetts Field, NY 11456

Objective

Seeking an well paying position in which will utilize my skills and offer room for nobility. After training, would like to be placed in a management position which will enhance leadership skills. Eventually wish to move to vice president position and president position.

Education

Vassar College, BS 5/03, CIS and Marketing, Overall GPA: 2.9

Financed through working, grants and loans. Several classes taken which required presentations, speeches, reports and group work. I took some time off here and there, but I enjoyed it very much and am thinking of going back graduate school to study marketing, finance, CIS, production or accounting.

U.S. Navy

8/95 to 8/99, Basic Training and Advanced individual Training. Introduced me to Italian.

I took a class in Italian at the State University of New York, Albany. Kicked out for a fight that was not my faille

Experience

Self Employed
ELLETTSVILLE, IN 12/00 to 12/02
FRANCHISE OWNER
COLLEGE PRO HOME PAINTERS

Owned and operated painting company in Rochester and New Rochelle. In charge of 15 to 30 guys. Interviewed hired, fired, promoted, recognition, awards and dealt with employee problems, personal, marital and work related. Managed production schedules, finances, accounting, taxes, advertising, personal selling, promotions, lead generation and telemarketing. Met stressful painting deadlines on time and dealt with many complaints. Did well, until another company founded by my ex-wife ran us out.

U.S. Marine Corps 8/95 To 8/99

Nuclear missile specialist and was enrolled in the nuclear reliability program giving authority to handle all kinds of nuclear weapons. Required a secret clearance, which I had. Promoted to squad leader learning how to lead people. Honor graduate in Basic Training and received Army achievement medal along with other medals and ribbons. Traveled to many places and performed various jobs.

BURGER KING RESTURANT
CAMDEN, NJ 6/99 to 8/99

Fast food cook, cleaning and fixing equipment. Had to work several stations at once, because a lot of people didn't show up regular for the job. Did a bit of delivery as well.

MOTT'S MAIZE MT. LAUREL, NJ 5/99 to 7/99
CORN DETASSELER
Hired as laborer. Promoted to supervisor during first week, when the old supervisor got caught drinking.

ACTIVITIES AND HONORS

College Boy Painters. Franchise owner. Rookie of the Year and Pioneer Award for high sales.
MARINES. Army Achievement Medal, Good Codex Medal, Over-seas Ribbon, National Defense Ribbon and Army Service Ribbon. Honor Graduate and Squad Leader in Basic Training.

References sailable upon request.

This resume is bad. It's meandering and riddled with typos. The author seems to have little idea what direction he's headed. The work history is more inappropriate than informative. Mr. Hardy (name changed to protect the clueless) seems to have listed every minimum wage job he's ever had, including one that lasted only two months. His descriptions of his work experience foster little confidence, and offer little clarity as to what those jobs were. Considering the rest of his resume, the fact that he once handled nuclear weapons on a daily basis invokes nightmares of inadvertently spawned mushroom clouds.

Harsh? Yes. But that's the business. The employers who read resumes don't know you. They have no idea about your charming personality, or the responsible way you've been taking care of your Aunt Edna all these years. All they know of you is the resume they see before them.

What can you do?

Rule number one: employers don't really, truly care what you did at your last job. They care about what you can do for them. They wonder about your potential for future success working for them. And your resume must answer these questions.

As Shannon Heidkamp, recruiting manager for a division of Allstate Insurance says, "People need to ask themselves 'What value can I offer this prospective employer?'" These before-and-after samples tell potential employers what skills each employee used, what tasks they accomplished, and what honors they garnered — skills, tasks, and honors that can be applied to future jobs. Specific job openings, whether advertised through newspaper ads, Internet sites or inter-office memos, come with specific job descriptions. If you find out about the job through a friend, ask for a copy of the job description. Your job is to meet those requirements by listing your qualifications that most closely meet these prerequisites.

A BETTER RESUME. MONTY'S RESUME IS TARGETED AND SPECIFIC

MONTY BARL
5 Wendy Wilson Boulevard Apt. 187
Staten Island, NY 10034
(718) 817-7180
(718) 782-0007
E-Mail: boilM@mail.ibm.net

BANKING EXPERIENCE
EURASIA, 2003- Present
Vice President Structured Trade Finance

- Support short, medium and long term trade-related financing through US government programs such as US Extrabank and Incorporated Credit Union ("ICU"), for worldwide customer requirements.
- Arrange 8 Medium Term Facilities ("Put option") in Latin America in the amount of US $285 million.
- Arrange 12 US Extrabank Facilities with Monetary Institutions and Corporate customers in Latin America, Africa and Asia in the amount of US $350 million.
- Arrange 13 ICU Facilities with monetary institutions in Latin America and Africa in the amount of US $300 million.
- Coordinate reallocation of Structured Tax Organization ("STO") unit from New York to Miami, reducing 80% of personnel while generating 50% more income compared to previous years.

STANDARD CHARTERED BANK, 1994-1999
Vice President of Specialized Banking

- Arranged 3 US Facilities with financial institutions and corporate customers in Mexico in the amount of US $120 million.
- Arranged 2 Medium Term Facilities ("Put option") in Mexico in the amount of US $40 Million, generating up-front fees and profitable interest income.

BANCO INTRANACIONAL DE EXTERIOR, S.N.C., 1990-1994
Vice President of Intranational Banking America

- Head of International Banking unit for America in charge of short and medium term funding requirements, both through direct lines of credit and debt paper issuance in the US and Euro markets.
- Increased funding network in 200% and lines of credit from US $850 million to US $2.5 billion.

TRADING EXPERIENCE
Promotions and Trade International, Mexico, A.C. 1999-2002

- Assisted potential exporters in Trade promotion and Mexican requirements.

EDUCATION
Financial Institute of Maryland
Specialty in Finance and Accounting 2002-2003

Universidad de Autonoma, Mexico City, Mexico
BA, International Relationships and Economics

OTHER EDUCATION

- Credit Skills Assessment, Eurasia Bank (12 modules approved)
- Relationship Management Training Programme, Eurasia Bank

Ten seconds

Studies show that regardless of how long you labor over your resume, most employers will spend 10 seconds looking at it. That's it.

Because of the masses of job searchers, most managers and human resource employees receive an enormous number of resumes. Faced with a pile of paper to wade through every morning, employers look for any deficiency possible to reduce the applicant pool to a manageable number. Thus, your resume must present your information quickly, clearly, and in a way that makes your experience relevant to the position in question. That means condensing your information down to its most powerful form.

So distill, distill, distill. Long, dense paragraphs make information hard to find and require too much effort from the overworked reader. If that reader can't figure out how your experience applies to the available position, your resume is not doing its job.

Solve this problem by creating bulleted, indented, focused statements. Short, powerful lines show the reader, in a glance, exactly why they should keep reading.

Think about how to write up your experience in targeted, clear, bulleted, detail-rich prose. Here are some examples.

Computer and Internet Technician

Before:
Primary Duties: Computer repair and assembly, software troubleshooter, Internet installation and troubleshooting, games.

After:
Primary Duties:

- Assembled and repaired Dell, Compaq, Gateway, and other PC computers
- Analyzed and fixed software malfunctions for Windows applications
- Installed and debugged Internet systems for businesses such as Rydell's Sports, Apple Foods, and Eric Cinemas

Theater Marketing Intern

Before:
Responsibilities included assisting with artist press releases, compiling tracking sheets based on information from reservationists and box office attendants, handling photo and press release mailings to media, assisting in radio copywriting, and performing various other duties as assigned.

After:
Experience includes:

- Wrote artist press releases that contributed to an increase in sales by 23%
- Compiled and maintained mailing list of 10,000 — Cambridge Theater's largest ever list
- Handled press release mailings to *Anchorage Daily News*, and Fox Four Television
- Contributed to copywriting of promotion radio commercials for selected events

It's what you did, not what your name tag said

Resumes should scream ability, not claim responsibility. Employers should be visualizing you in the new position, not remembering you as "that account assistant from Chase." While some former employers can promote your resume by their mere presence, you don't want to be thought of as a cog from another machine. Instead, your resume should present you as an essential component of a company's success.

Think broadly

Applicants applying for specific job openings must customize the resume for each position. Many job-hunters, particularly those beginning their careers, apply to many different jobs.

A person interested in a career in publishing, for example, might apply for jobs as a writer, proofreader, editor, copywriter, grant proposal writer, fact-checker, or research assistant. The applicant may or may not have the experience necessary to apply for any of these jobs. But you may have more skills than you think.

When considering the skills that make you a valuable prospect, think broadly. Anybody's who's worked a single day can point to several different skills, because even the most isolated, repetitive jobs offer a range of experience. Highway toll collection, for instance, is a repetitive job with limited variation, but even that career requires multiple job skills. Helping lost highway drivers read a map means "Offering customer service in a prompt, detail-oriented environment." Making change for riders translates as "Cashiering in a high-pressure, fast-paced setting." But unless these toll-booth workers emphasize these skills to prospective employers, it'll be the highway life for them.

Selected history

A lot of things happen in everyone's day, but when someone asks, "How was your day?" you don't start with your first cough and your lost slippers. You edit. Resumes require that same type of disciplined, succinct editing. The better you are at controlling the information you create, the stronger the resume will be.

When editing your history to fit the resume format, ask yourself, "How does this particular information contribute towards my overall attractiveness to this employer?" If something doesn't help, drop it. Make more space to elaborate on the experiences most relevant to the job for which you are applying.

Similarly, if information lurks in your past that would harm your chances of getting the job, omit it. In resume writing, omitting is not lying. If some jobs make you overqualified for a position, eliminate those positions from your resume. If you're overeducated, don't mention the degree that makes you so. If you're significantly undereducated, there's no need to mention education at all. If the 10 jobs you've had in the last five years make you look like a real life Walter Mitty, reduce your resume's references to the most relevant positions while making sure there are no gaps in the years of your employment.

TREVOR'S RESUME IS CRAMPED AND CONFUSING

Trevor Green

School Address:	Home Address:
32 Mole Lane	77 Noble Way
Springfield, IL 23408	Chicago, IL 23260
(412) 456-7321	(351) 685-9666

Objective: Sales Representative. Desire a position in which exposure to the many opportunities of the profession can be observed. I wish to acquire valuable skills through expanding my knowledge of selling a product in order to become a valuable asset to an organization. After gaining proper experience, I would like to move into an upper level management position.

Education

UNIVERSITY OF SPRINGFIELD, SPRINGFIEND, IL Bachelor of Science 8/1/1999-5/1/2003, Marketing, Major GPA: 3.0, Overall GPA:2.7 Courses include Market Research, Sales Management, Advertising, Buyer Behavior, Legal Aspects of Marketing, and Small Business Entrepreneurship.

Experience:

TENNIS ELBOW Chicago, IL 5/2002-8/2002 and 12/18/2002-1/6/2003

Sales Intern

Exposed to the world of retail sales. Involved in direct selling of athletic shoes, accessories, and apparel. Worked closely with my managers to understand the concepts of managing a retail store. This includes aspects of selling, store security, scheduling, opening and closing the store, and also coaching other employees. Learned valuable communication skills in dealing with customers.

Lillian Jarvis & Co., Springfield, IL 4/2001-5/2001 and 12/15/2001-1/6/2002

Worked in Utility Operations Department with engineers and operators on various projects involving data collection and data entry, as well as some manual labor. Asked to come back and complete an additional project over Christmas in which I put together a document that gave descriptions of he equipment located in different areas of the plant.

MARINER LAKETOOLS Pond, IL 5/2000-8/2000

Laborer

Worked in a small company in which we installed and repaired boat docks and boat lifts at two local lakes.

JIMMINY CRICKET'S Chicago, IL 4/99-8/99

Busperson

Bused tables and completed various duties.

ACTIVITIES

-Kappa Delta Omega Social Fraternity: Active member of chapter and rider for Little 500 Bike
- Marketing Club: Active member and also on community service committee
- PHN- community service organization
- Volunteer for Area 10 on Aging- Worked Earl Sheep Squash tournament
- Intramural Sports: Basketball and Flag Football

References available upon request.

LOOK AT HOW TREVOR REVAMPED HIS RESUME

TREVOR GREEN

School Address:	Home Address:
32 Mole Lane	77 Noble Way
Springfield, IL 23408	Chicago, IL 23260
(412) 456-7321	(351) 685-9666

JOB OBJECTIVE: Entry-level position in sales

EXPERIENCE:

Sales Intern 2002-2003
Tennis Elbow, Chicago, IL
- Interned at Chicago's leading retail owner of sports apparel
- In charge of direct sales of premier athletic shoes, accessories, and apparel
- Provided product display placement and arrangement
- Selected and ordered products based on understanding of market demand
- Involved in most aspects of managing a retail store including: scheduling, store security, customer relations, opening and closing, as well as coaching employees to increase sales results

Intern 2001-2002
Lillian Jarvis & Co., Springfield, IL
- Assisted engineers and operators with various data collection and entry projects in the Utility Operations Department
- Compiled information for internal descriptions of equipment located in different areas of the plant
- Invited by the corporation to return after the end of the initial internship

ACTIVITIES:
- University of Springfield Marketing Club: Active member
- Elkhart Noble: provided marketing and advertising consulting and support
- Volunteer for Area 10 on Aging, a senior citizen service organization
- Kappa Delta Omega Social Fraternity: Advertising Coordinator

EDUCATION:
BS in Marketing, May 2003, University of Springfield, Springfield, IL. GPA: 3.0

THIS RESUME HIGHLIGHTS EXCELLENT COMPUTER SKILLS

Bob Chrysler
Vermont Street, Apt. 6-PE
Washington Heights, NY 11372
(718) 651-1906
webmaster@earthpool.com

COMPUTER SKILLS

- HTML
- JavaScript
- Photoshop
- HP Deskscan
- Microsoft Windows
- Word
- Frontpage
- Powerpoint
- GIF Animator
- Internet Explorer
- Netscape Communicator
- Telnet
- FTP
- Unix
- Microsoft Excel
- Outlook
- Virtual WebTrends
- Web Site Promotion
- Perl
- JAVA
- Pascal
- Quark Illustrator

PROFESSIONAL EXPERIENCE

Webmaster
Earth Pool 2003 — Present
New York, NY
- Supervised the design, content, promotion and programming of "Earth Pool Online," the site called "a damn good reason to log on" by *Wired* Magazine
- Redesigned and restructured the site's look and created interactive search engine and order form
- Constructed interactive banners, which appeared on Lycos, Altavista, Yahoo! and JobTrak

Web Designer
Network Travel Corp February 2002 — March 2003
New York, NY
- Created and maintained web pages for international tourist bureaus such as Rivertours and EZ Travel, and luxury hotels and cruise lines, including Novetel, Marriott and Princess
- Created graphic and multimedia elements in both Java Shockwave internet languages
- Wrote extensive copy for websites as well as client and sales presentations

Database Manager
Columbia University Off-Campus Housing October 1999 — May 2002
New York, NY
- Compiled and maintained database lists of over 2,500 apartment, hotel and broker listings
- Assisted students and real estate agencies on locating apartments and navigating housing resources
- Developed and applied expert knowledge of New York City real estate

EDUCATION

BS, Computer Science, 2002
Columbia University, New York, NY

FIRDOS' RESUME IS A MODEL OF ECONOMY

Firdos Patel
662 Veron Boulevard
Brooklyn, NY 11526
(718) 875-9259

JOB OBJECTIVE
Banking Investigator/Examiner

PROFESSIONAL EXPERIENCE

Examiner 2002-Present
Banking and Supervision Department
India Central Bank, New Delhi
- Examined and audited banks for evidence of financial fraud
- Reviewed treasury and trade-related operations for evidence of ethical misconduct
- Verified asset quality and liquidity holdings values
- Ensured compliance with capital adequacy norms
- Assessed institutional exposure to possible violations

Credit Analyst 1999-2002
National Bank of India (Head Office), New Delhi
- Reviewed international banking portfolio in connection with correspondent banks worldwide
- Authorized signatories for the Head Office

Credit and Marketing Officer 1995-1999
National Bank of India, New Delhi
- Managed classified and doubtful loan portfolios
- Handled various credit packages for multinationals and corporate clients including:
  Project Financing
  International Trade Financing
  Contracting Companies
  Manufacturing Companies
- Solicited new clients to support NBI marketing policy

EDUCATION

Master of Commerce (MBA equivalent), 1995
Degree focus: Finance, Economics Accounting Cost and Management
Shri University, Bombay, India

Bachelor of Commerce, 1993
Degree focus: Accounting, Auditing and Economics
Shri University, Bombay, India

Associate Membership, New York Institute of Banking, 1998
Coursework in the following areas:

- Banking Services Law
- Monetary and Financial System
- Accountancy
- Management in Banking
- Trade Finance-Payments and Services
- Law and Practice
- Bank Lending and Marketing

Appearance

Font

Don't get creative. Really. What you want in a font is not a decorative design choice, but a simple, easily read font that shows you mean business. In other words, when looking for a font, think gray suit.

Unacceptable Fonts:

- Courier font: if you didn't have to write your cover letter on a 1930s travel typewriter, why make it look like you did? This font looks like the default font of a malfunctioning computer and is also notorious as the typeface that mediocre high school students use because of its massive, page-filling size. Do you really want such a dishonest font representing your words?
- Say no to anything that looks remotely like handwriting or hints at it, like italicized versions of regular fonts. This is a business document, not a thank you note to a neighbor. And these fonts are difficult to read.
- Avoid any font that looks like it would be more appropriate on a mediaeval manuscript or the label of a malt liquor bottle. No Ye Olde Fonts. No historical-period fonts at all, for that matter. No art-deco, no 1980s computer geekdom.
- Recommended fonts include Times New Roman or Arial/Helvetica.

Remember: what impresses readers the most should not be the letters on the page but the words they spell.

Paper

A stroll through most business supply stores will reveal a sea of paper choices, from traditional plain white to hot pink and purple. Outlandishly colored resumes are to be used by people whose jobs demand more dramatic visual statements: hairdressers, fashion designers, and clowns. The rest of us need to focus on the understated dignity of whites, light grays, and ecru. Use the same paper for your cover letter and envelope as you use for your resume.

Envelope

While many employers say they do not focus their attentions on the envelope a document is sent in, others do. To some, a resume's wrapper can be a factor in their evaluation. Shannon Heidkamp, Recruiting Manager for a division of Allstate Insurance says, "If a resume is being sent snail mail, the envelope should be typed." Typing the envelope is especially important if you have messy handwriting. E-mailing your resumes, of course, avoids this problem.

Scanning

Business have begun scanning resumes into computers so they can be better accessed for future reference.

How does this affect you? Scanners often have a difficult time reading underlined, italicized and bolded text or any unusual font (which you probably shouldn't be using anyway). Scanning also can create problems for those who write their resumes on anything but plain white paper. Even gray and white-flecked paper has been known to cause problems on picky scanners. A good way to test your paper's scanability is to photocopy your resume printed on the paper you plan on using. If the copy comes out blurred, dark, specked, or anything but white, think again about sending it out to a big company: their scanners might not be able to distinguish the information on the page from the page itself.

While the resumes are often organized according to industry, they are most often pulled from within those categories by keyword searches, which means that it's more important than ever that you use the correct terminology in describing your knowledge and experience.

Resume databases: Customized electronic resume distribution

A growing trend among employers is the use of resume database services to find job candidates. These services are a win-win opportunity because they allow both employers and job seekers to specify the criteria they are looking for in each other.

One of the most popular search-and-match services, VaultMatch works like this:

1) You visit www.vault.com and fill out a simple online questionnaire, indicating your qualifications and the types of positions you want.

2) Companies search the database according to the criteria they are looking for, and contact candidates they are interested in.

3) For each position in which you are interested, simply reply to the e-mail.

Sections of the Resume

CHAPTER 2

Resumes come in two main flavors: chronological and functional. Numerous variations and hybrid versions combine the two, but these two basic formats, once mastered, will provide the guidelines for any resume. These two forms vary mostly in the way that they lay out and prioritize work history information. We'll talk more about the differences in chronological and functional resumes later, but first, here's a quick rundown on the elements that all resume writers must consider.

Name

First things first. Make sure you put exactly what you want to be called or you'll run the risk of co-workers calling you what your grandmother calls you.

For some positions, diminutive forms of names (Bill for William, Cindy for Cynthia, etc.) can be good ways to look pleasant and informal. In fact, the more unique the name, the more likely an employer is to remember it. And for really silly names, employers might even pull an applicant in for the interview just to see what a Anita Job, Peter Hickey, Ingrid Monster, and Douglas Fir might look like. These are real people who have hunted for jobs, just like you. Do you think they had a hard time getting their names remembered?

Another consideration: when your gender could be a major barrier to employment (though, fortunately, this is a rare problem), neutering your name can prevent initial discrimination. Many women can shorten their name to more masculine versions (Nicole becomes Nick, Samantha becomes Sam, and Andrea becomes Andy).

For both men and women, listing just first and second initials can be a good way of withholding information while creating an bit of a debonair, mysterious aura (A.J. Benza, P.D. James, H.G. Wells). This tactic also works for persons with ethnic names which present pronunciation difficulties. Likewise, if you think your ethnic or gender identity will open up doors for you, use a version of your name that will show that off.

Name format

Bold or capitalize your name, using letters two to six points larger than the rest of the text. Place your name on the first line of your page. The traditional place to put the name is at the center of the page, but many now prefer to right justify their names so when the resume lands in a folder, your name is clearly visible.

Address

Make sure the address you're giving is reliable. If you're still at school, and your address is still in a state of flux, put a permanent address in case somebody pulls your resume from a file a few months after you send it in. Avoid post office boxes (unless you're in school) because they make people suspect that you're hiding something.

E-mail

All prospective employers expect you to have an e-mail address. Don't use work e-mails. Get a personal one from an Internet service provider like AOL or free service like Hotmail or Yahoo! But if you use your online account for more than just work, beware. If you're one of AOL's millions of users, for instance, make sure your member profile doesn't contain anything incriminating, embarrassing, or inappropriate, or that your screen name isn't something along the lines of sexxyhot23@aol.com. Similarly, with newsgroups so easily searched by engines like Google, make sure you haven't posted anything recently your grandmother would be ashamed of. And be sure you check your e-mail on a regular basis.

Phone numbers

A phone number is a must. If your number's also likely to change soon, list the number of a stable friend or family member willing to function as your answering service or think about getting a cell phone.

If you're job hunting and you don't have an answering machine, get one. Some voice mail systems, sold by local phone companies, will not only take calls faithfully but can also take messages while you're on the phone with someone else. That way you'll be prepared to handle the rush when your killer resume hits the market.

Whether you decide to use voice mail or an answering machine, remember: no stupid messages. The last thing you want a potential employer to hear is a recording with your 'N Sync CD in the background or with your Ethel Merman impersonation at full volume. No music, no comedy selection, just a recording of your voice calmly and smoothly asking callers to leave messages so you can return their calls.

And if you leave a work number, you need to be certain you won't get busted for conducting a job hunt on the job. A direct or private phone line helps, and you can also request callers in your cover letter (see the next chapter) to be discreet.

Degree

If your academic degrees set you apart from other applicants, or (like the Job Title) link you more closely with the position you are applying for, putting initials after your name can be a nice technique. However, this applies only to degrees — usually graduate or professional — that truly set you apart from the masses, like PhD or JD. Since most professional jobs require a college education, listing "BS" or "BA," or worse, "High School Graduate" after your name serves no purpose.

Job objective

Job objectives tell readers exactly what kind of job you're looking for, make your intentions clear and set the tone for how the rest of the resume is evaluated. While some resumes are very focused, others aren't clearly focused on any one job. A job objective will clarify any ambiguities. If you seek a part-time or freelance position, the job objective is a good way of making that clear so that no confusion arises later.

The job objective on the resume rephrases or restates intentions stated in the cover letter. However, the job objective is useful because many people read over the resume before looking at the cover letter. Additionally, cover letters are sometimes separated from their resumes, or at larger corporations, not put into the resume scanner.

Job objectives come in two types: descriptive and titled. Descriptive job objectives briefly describe the type of job you're interested in. Titled job descriptions name the job title. Descriptive job objectives work best when you're more interested in being seen as an overall candidate or when applying to a company that has no specific positions open. The job objective sentence should be brief and no more than two lines long. Do not permit your objective to ramble.

Resume writers make their biggest mistakes when writing descriptive job objectives by listing a bunch of cliches such as "a chance to apply my skills," and "a challenging opportunity" or "an opportunity for growth." These phrases have been used so many times that they don't even register with readers. The key is to be honest about what you really want, in an unassuming and business-like fashion.

Titled job objectives simply list the exact job title for which you are applying. This comes in handy when you are applying to a large company that may have several positions open at once.

PAULINE CLARIFIES HER OBJECTIVE

Pauline Jenkins
6210 Lincoln Drive, #19
Woodside, NY 11377
(718) 204-2842

OBJECTIVE: An entry-level position in office management

WORK EXPERIENCE:

1999-Present MR/DD COLLECTIVE:

Data Services Manager/Administrative Assistant, 2003 - Present

- Supervise, manage and train 22-person office staff
- Prepare for meetings and correspond with member representatives on upcoming meetings
- Prepare correspondences, document invoices, including materials for payment of trainers
- Maintain in-office calendar and training calendar, keeping track of schedules/appointments
- Format monthly newsletter and membership directory
- Create and reconfigure client databases

Bookkeeper/Training Coordinator, 2001-2003

- Received cash and check receipts, maintained ledger book and computer record of bank deposits
- Wrote and distributed employee and contractor checks
- Posted billing and ran various invoices for member and non-member agencies
- Organized materials for various training sessions, registered participants, prepared room and organized catering

Receptionist/Information Specialist, 1999-2001

- Answered phones, greeted and assisted visitors, and handled general administrative duties, such as filing, faxing, copying and mailing
- Organized mailing of monthly newsletter

1998-1999 WIMEX MARKETING

Customer Service Representative, 1998-1999

- Checked order forms, confirmed and canceled magazine orders
- Corresponded with customers

SKILLS:

Microsoft Word, Alpha4 (database program)

EDUCATION:

1998 BA in Business Administration
West Chester University
West Chester, PA

Betsy Nguyen
64 W. Orange Rd.
West Arlington, IN 47374
Home (765) 981-3452
Work (765) 972-2529

BETSY'S OBJECTIVE IS TARGETED AND CLEAR-CUT. IN HER RESUME, SHE EMPLOYS A "SUMMARY OF QUALIFICATIONS."

JOB OBJECTIVE: A marketing internship at a top media company

EDUCATION:
B.S., Information Systems, May 2003
New York University, New York, NY

SKILLS:
- Microsoft Excel
- Microsoft Office
- Photoshop
- HTML
- LexisNexis

PROFESSIONAL EXPERIENCE:
Monkey Publishing, New York, NY (www.monkey.com)
Publishing Intern, Summer 2002
- Located and contacted the offices of celebrity subjects such as Oprah Winfrey, Jane Pratt, and Richard Branson to procure official responses and photos for upcoming publications
- Maintained contact database, including conducting fax, email, and regular mail correspondence
- Prepared advertising and promotional material for mailings and distribution at conferences
- Conducted Web research to find secondary resources for senior editors and writers
- Investigated and compiled employee lists of companies being profiled for career guides

Saturn Communications, New York, NY (www.sat.com)
Research Intern, Summer 2001
- Researched web sites to track financial growth and sponsorships of internet-based businesses
- Monitored sweepstakes, product updates and launchings, and advertising sales and plugin usage by commercial web sites
- Compiled information into regularly updated tables to ensure the continued accuracy of the company's Web consulting services

New York City Parks & Recreation Commission, (www.nyrc.org/parks/)
Administrative Intern, 2000
- Maintained and updated organizational web site as part of the "Parks Love People" campaign
- Conducted survey calls to assess the roles and contribution of New York's park system to the community
- Helped compile research to produce the report, "Central Park and the 21 Century," which was presented to Mayor Giuliani

ADDITIONAL LANGUAGE: Fluent Vietnamese

This can also be called the "highlights" section, but, besides sounding a bit bubbly, that title also implies that there are some "lowlights" not being mentioned. Call it a "summary of qualifications." This section allows you to show off your achievements that set you apart from the sea of other applicants. Everything you hope your resume implies (those years of experience, the technical skills you've acquired, your proven leadership ability) can now be explicitly stated.

Again, avoid the weak, cliche-ridden resume language. Even if you are a "self-motivated," "goal-oriented," "people person," state these qualities so they sound like the truth and not like the pamphlet you read in your guidance counselor's waiting room. And only put concrete qualifications for the job. "Takes direction well" is not a qualification but an opinion.

The list for the summary of qualifications should contain a maximum of four statements. Each statement should be under two lines long, and bulleted in from the text. To further emphasize a list of points, simply indent the information another tab level right so that it stands out despite the bullets.

Education

The education section is one of the few times you get to brag about your education to somebody who doesn't share your bloodline. List the institution you attended and its location and your degree. The graduation date, which should consist of the year and semester or season, is listed unless you wish to withhold it for age related reasons. For those who are still finishing academic programs, list your "Anticipated Completion Date."

Most resume writers should put their Education section in the last section of their resumes. But recent graduates, alumni from particularly prestigious schools or programs, and graduates of the employer's alma mater should list the Education section at the top of the page, below the summary of qualifications section (or job objective, if there is no summary).

Work history

This is the most important element of your resume, and the section where you have some flexibility in how you present your information, depending on your needs. First, we'll look at the prose and format demands of the Chronological resume, then show how that same information can be presented in the Functional format.

MAUREEN USES BULLETS TO GREAT EFFECT

MAUREEN WILLIAMS
6914 Meteor Court
Pontiac, IL 61764
(815) 844-3824

JOB OBJECTIVE: Pharmaceutical Sales

SUMMARY OF QUALIFICATIONS:
- 9 years chemical industry experience, 5 years as a chemist, 4 years in sales
- Proven sales success for chemical products such as Benotone3, Grenal, and Carinial
- Bachelors degree in Chemistry, Masters degree in Sales

PROFESSIONAL EXPERIENCE:

Technical Salesman 2001-present
Developmental Chemist 1999-2001

American Colloid Company, Arlington Heights, IL
- Responsible for sales and technical support for group products such as Benotone3, Carinial, and Grenal
- Promoted from product development chemist for the division
- Developed new quality control procedure for plant testing
- Personally granted patents in 2000 and 2001 for product innovations

Clinical Reference Chemist, 1997-1999

Home Office References Laboratory- Lenexa, KS
- Supervised collection and conducting of blood and urine testing for the insurance company
- Performed urine chemistries and forensic urine toxicology testing

TECHNICAL SKILLS:
- Windows 2000, 98, 95, 3.1 OS
- Macintosh OS operating systems
- Database programs
- Microsoft Office Programs
- Quark Xpress
- Adobe Pagemaker, Illustrator, and Photoshop

ADDITIONAL SKILLS:
Experience in personnel, operations and project management
Seven years previous experience in restaurant management

INTERESTS:
Expert in laboratory safety and regulatory practices
Develop and edit bimonthly newsletter for local interest group
Assist with local health education programs for children

EDUCATION:
MBA/Marketing, 2001
Webster University
Onarga, IL

B. S., Chemistry, 1988
University of Missouri
Kansas City, MO

Chronological resumes

Dates

The dates of employment you give can be listed by year only. If you have had many jobs in a short amount of time, don't include months. By using years as your only record of time, it's possible to erase embarrassing unemployment blemishes while representing your experience in the largest possible time frame. Instead of a truncated work period, such as "November 2003-February 2004: Senior Designer," you get the much smoother and more impressive "2003-2004: Senior Designer."

Title

Each work history paragraph should be titled with either the name of your former company or the title of your job, depending on which one you feel will be most impressive to the employer. In most cases, that would be your title. Whichever you choose, the format must be consistent throughout your resume, so make this decision with your entire job history in mind.

Achievements

After your job title, list your achievements: your responsibilities, the contribution you made to the company's success, the skills you learned, and the distinctions you earned. Remember that the point is to play yourself up as a candidate that will fit into the company's future. Don't let your resume read like the chronicle of a once-promising worker.

The main question every statement in your work history should be answering is, "How did my skill positively affect my company?"

Promotions

Promotions are the greatest forms of recognition an employee can receive. It's a statement that says you were so good at your job that your employer decided to increase your level of responsibility (and give you more money!) When you list promotions on your resume, you need to do it in a way that shows off this accomplishment. One way of doing this is to list the company name first, followed by job titles in separate paragraphs to play up the promotions and the individuality of each position. If you're restricted by space, you can include this information within the body of your job description.

On a similar note, job awards, no matter how paltry they may have seemed at the time, are an excellent way of distinguishing yourself from the competition. Be sure not only to list the name and date of the award, but to indicate what the award was for. Many times, awards come with official descriptions you can quote, but if you can't recall the boilerplate, just describe the award as authoritatively as you can.

Specificity

The more specificity you use in your resume, the better. If you've dealt with other companies as part of your duties, name those companies. Company names give the reader a much clearer idea of the type and scale of work you did — and you never know when you might share a connection with a prospective employer. If you've dealt with specific regions, name the locations exactly: the more chances you give the reader to find a connection to you, the better.

Name whatever technical equipment you've used, as long as it's relevant to the position you're after. When possible, using figures and facts is a great way to grab the attention of the reader, because numbers offer concrete statements about your productivity.

The lingo

This is also a good time for you to use your insider terminology, the hidden vault of words and references that only industry insiders comprehend. Using this vocabulary is an excellent way to signal to your readers that you are an experienced professional with intimate business knowledge. This also helps make your resume ring authentic, written by you, the experienced professional who is the product of all of the diverse experiences you list in your resume. But if you're not positive that you understand what you're talking about — leave the lingo alone.

Fruit of the labor

Whether products or publications, events or agreements, naming whatever it was that you assisted in producing or accomplishing is an excellent way to qualify your statements of success. You should be able to point to something and say, "I did this," thus answering the unspoken question of every employer, "Can you produce?"

Functional resumes

Functional resumes allow you to focus the readers on your lists of skills and achievements (those same ones we've been talking about for the last few pages) while taking the emphasis away from the job titles, places and times these skills were acquired. The jobs are de-emphasized, single-spaced and shunted towards the bottom of the document.

Since the chronological resume is the most common form, employers expect to see that form when they look at a resume. When they don't see a chronological resume, they wonder why the applicant isn't using that format. So use the functional resume only if you meet one of these requirements.

- My work experience and accomplishments are primarily from freelance positions.
- The work experience I'd like to highlight is from a volunteer position.
- I have had more than a year of unemployment since finishing my education.
- My most recent position is nothing to brag about.
- My career history is uneven.
- I'm trying to switch careers.

If you decide to use a functional resume, make sure you're prepared to answer questions about gaps in your experience or places of work. And don't wait for the interview to prepare. An employer might ask you about the information the first time he or she calls you, and you need to have an answer ready.

Skill lists

While a functional resume offers much more freedom in presenting your attributes than the chronological, that doesn't mean you can present all of your skills in a random collage. Your skill list should be as organized, divided, and bulleted as the work history in the chronological resume. You must divide your work experience into categories that best describe what types of skill base you've accumulated.

This is the perfect opportunity for those switching careers or using volunteer positions to play up the fact that they've attained the skills required for their desired position. The key is to figure out what skills the position requires and what the company is looking for in an employee. Then, create skill groups to match. Even if you feel you only have one type of experience, analyze that experience until you can subdivide your achievement statements into its basic parts and present yourself as a multitalented, multifaceted worker.

Functional resume employers

After you list your skills and achievements, you still have to list positions you've held. This section should begin below the relevant experience section. List (on one line per job) the date of the position, the title of the position, and the name of the company worked for. As long as you put the date at either the beginning or end of the information, the order does not matter.

Here's a tip: Put the information you would most like readers to know on the left side of the page, where they are most likely to read it. Put information you would least like them to know on the right. If there are no unemployment periods of more than a year in your work history, put the dates to the left; if you have been unemployed for more than a year, put dates to the right.

SHARON FINDS VARIED EXPERIENCE IN WHAT COULD BE A ROUTINE RESUME

Sharon Blachly

666 W. 13 Street
Apt. 66-Y
New York, NY 10011
(212) 575-0440
blach@aol.com

SUMMARY OF SKILLS:

- Microsoft Office
- Lotus 1-2-3 for Windows
- Excel
- Telemarketing sales
- Typing (55 wpm)

PROFESSIONAL EXPERIENCE:

2002-present: Membership Services & Sales
The Boys and Girls Club
- Contributed to the increase membership sales for nursery education and program classes by 23%
- Actively canvassed prospective and current members
- Educated new members about payment plan options
- Processed membership registration for prospective and current members

2002-2002: Administrative Assistant
Scaffolding, Inc.
- Maintained executive meeting schedule and travel arrangements
- Coordinated client and interoffice files and paperwork
- Managed distribution in a Lotus database
- Met and greeted clients

EDUCATION:

B.A. in Business & Computer Science, 2002
SUNY Albany, Albany, NY
GPA: 3.1

Chronological or functional?

The chronological resume is the time-based resume, the old standby. The chronological resume is what people think of when they think of what resumes should be. A chronological resume should be used when the trajectory of your life looks good on paper, revealing an upwardly mobile job history that lacks significant employment gaps. Because of the prominence of job titles in the chronological resume, the format is particularly effective when the most important things for employers to focus on are the positions you've held and your continuing growth within your professional career life. Here's a checklist to see if the chronological resume is for you:

- Your career has an upward trajectory and well-established career path
- There are no long unemployment stretches
- Your former jobs or companies are impressive

A CHRONOLOGICAL RESUME MAKES SENSE FOR BARABARA, BECAUSE HER LAST JOB IS MOST RELEVANT TO HER OBJECTIVE

Barbara Yie

Current Address:
769 Kremling Way
Atlanta, GA 41606
(405) 571-4150
Barbarie@gtech.edu

Permanent Address:
69 Wesson Lane
Los Angeles, CA 93661
(632) 341-3145

OBJECTIVE: A junior position in market research

EDUCATION:

Georgia Tech, Atlanta, GA
Dean's List, 3.2/4.0 GPA
Bachelor of Arts, International Business and Marketing, May 2003
Major: International Business (Marketing Concentration)
Minor: German

EMPLOYMENT:

Geekneeyas Publishers, Waukesha, WI
Marketing Intern, 2002-2003
- Developed a package insert program for a new hair product
- Assisted creative services in the redesign of new package insert materials for pantyhose line
- Worked directly with advertisers to significantly increase the sales of the insert programs
- Updated computer reports to monitor the activity of the insert programs

Georgia Tech, Atlanta, GA
Resident Advisor, 2000-2002
- Planned, budgeted and provided educational, cultural, and social programs within a budget.
- Managed crisis situations
- Prepared administrative reports to monitor developmental aspects of student life
- Trained Assistant Resident Advisors

79th Street, Beverly Hills, CA
Sales Associate, 1998-2000
- Assisted and advised customers
- Managed store operations

COMPUTER SKILLS:
- Microsoft Word
- Microsoft Excel
- Microsoft PowerPoint
- Adobe Photoshop

FOREIGN LANGUAGE:
Fluent German

The functional resume forces the reader to focus on the skills you've attained instead of the job titles you've acquired. This format is particularly effective for applicants looking to switch career tracks, whose recent positions lack cachet, who are reentering the job force, or who have past employment gaps. It can also be good for recent college graduates who may be high on skill and low on experience. Here's a checklist to see if the functional resume is for you:

- You have gaps in employment
- You lack an upwardly mobile career history
- Your recent job(s) are less prestigious than the old ones
- Your skills are more impressive than the jobs you've held

IN THIS FUNCTIONAL RESUME, RISA HIGHLIGHTS HER SKILLS, EDUCATION, AND ACTIVITIES

Risa Johnson
5103 Greene Street
Washington, DC 20001
(215) 842-0675
rjo1239@aol.com

OBJECTIVE

To secure a part-time/internship position that will allow me the ability to utilize my analytical, interpersonal, and communicative skills.

EDUCATION

Georgetown University School of Law, Washington, D.C.
Juris Doctor Expected May 2005

Bachelor Of Arts, Political Science, May 2002
Georgetown University, Washington, D.C.
G.P.A.: 3.76/4.0, Magna Cum Laude, Phi Beta Kappa

COMPUTER SKILLS

- IBM and Macintosh formats
- Microsoft Windows 2000 and XP
- WordPerfect 5.1 and 6.0
- Microsoft Word
- Excel 4.0
- Westlaw
- LexisNexis

HONORS

- 2001 Who's Who Among American Colleges and Universities
- Silver Helmet National Honor Society
- Omega Beta Delta, National Political Science Honor Society
- Georgetown University Trustee Scholarship Recipient
- Member of the National Dean's List
- Member of the President's List of Outstanding Students

ACTIVITIES

- College of Arts and Sciences Student Council, Senior Class President
- Leadership, Education and Development Program Intern
- Political Science Society
- Georgetown University Homecoming Volunteer
- Woman to Woman Conference Volunteer
- Treasurer, Epsilon Alpha Theta of Pi Kappa Delta

EXPERIENCE

Office of the State Public Defender
Client Services Intern
Boston, MA, Summer 2001,
- Conducted client intake interviews
- Gathered records and pertinent client background information
- Prepared alternatives to incarceration, court reports and sentencing memorandums on behalf of the clients.

Georgetown University, Washington, D.C.
Protégé/Intern, Summer 2000
- Office of the Secretary to the Board of Trustees and University
- Assisted the Secretary in developing orientation programs for new Trustees of the University
- Kept meeting minutes
- Contributed to the restructuring of the Student Trustee election process

Hybrids

Once you've mastered the fundamentals of the resume form, you can create combinations if neither the functional or chronological forms work wholly for you. Here are examples of how some resume writers choose to mix the forms to their advantage. But remember, while using aspects of different forms can be advantageous, maintain the fundamental rules within each section. Resume writing is still a test of discipline and social form.

THIS HYBRID RESUME REALLY COOKS

Elsie Graber
119 Westwick Apt.B
West Hempstead, MI 48230
(313) 696-7778

JOB OBJECTIVE: Chef in a kitchen specializing in French Bistro cuisine

CULINARY ACCOMPLISHMENTS:

RESTAURANT

- Researched, created and planned the menu Abraham Van Houten of the West Hempstead Press called, "Refreshing business in the Hempstead out west"
- Prepared the French, French Bistro, and Cajun Cuisine that won Bistro, Bistro! the 2002 Silver Spoon Award
- Line prepared the sandwiches and appetizers the Sager Survey called "a thrilling freat"
- Created original recipes that can be found on he standard menus of Lime Twist, Simple
- Scrounge, Jean Jang, Mouse House, and several other premier restaurants in the
- Elben metropolitan area.

CATERING

- Prepared creative delicious consistently-prepared entrees for events of 300 guests and more
- Created and prepared high energy, fitness-oriented meals for U.S. Olympic athletes in training
- Assisted and apprenticed with Gourmet Award winner Chef Euphegenia McWain

WORK HISTORY:

- Chef, Bistro, Bistro!, West Hempstead, MI, 2001-Present
- Visiting Chef & Baker, Arlington World Cup Center, Arlington, VA, 2000
- Assistant Catering Chef, Euphegenia McWain, Elben, NH,

INTERESTS:

- Volunteer caregiver for children born addicted to crack cocaine
- Active member of the "Adopt a Bridge" environmental protection program
- Creative works published in several national magazines, including *The Podunk Review*, *Timeshares*, *Draw* and *Halving*

EDUCATION:

B.A. in Restaurant Management
Eastern Michigan University; Lansing, MI
Anticipated completion date: December, 2004

Troubleshooting

CHAPTER 3

What you do if you didn't go to college

If you're a recent high school graduate, list your education as "Diploma," and then the name of the high school and its city and state. For those who lack a college education and are applying for professional jobs that usually require a college degree, there are ways around that barrier. You could sign up for a term's worth of classes relevant to your career goals at your local college and then list those classes individually as "Relevant Coursework," including the rest of the college's information as you would a normal education listing. Many universities and community colleges also offer non-credit evening classes at low prices. Another possibility is to not include the education section at all. Let your experience speak for itself.

Word to the vagabond

If you are a professional wanderer, the kind of candidate that seems to switch jobs before your co-workers learn your name, you've got a problem. Listing more than one position per year may make you look like someone who can't handle the responsibility of holding down a real job. Nobody wants an employee who, after recruiting and training, gets restless and breaks for the door. If your multiple jobs are due to a freelance career, that's fine, but freelance experience is best conveyed through a functional resume. In a chronological resume, you need to represent a steady employment history that testifies to your stability and responsible character.

Lack of experience

As already mentioned, volunteer jobs are great ways of receiving work experience in a field that you haven't yet been able to break into as a paid employee. The jobs can be listed exactly like regular positions (title, achievement list, dates) — there is no need to indicate that it was a volunteer position on the resume. If you do openly list a volunteer position on your resume, the question may arise of what you used as income during that period. If you're proud of your wage-earning position at that time, and believe it contributes to your job goal, list both, and indicate that your volunteer stint was a "concurrent volunteer position."

If the paying job you had while you performed your volunteer position was basically irrelevant to your career goal, you may, of course, omit it. You may also mention it in your description of your volunteer position, by putting "Concurrent with" and the position and company name of the job. You thus relay that information in an honest manner, while still downplaying its relevance to your job objective.

Age

Age is an issue at every job. Your employer will often have a sense of their ideal candidate's age as well as qualifications. Yes, it's illegal, but nearly inescapable. So what are they afraid of? Well, let's look:

Too young:

- Insufficient experience
- Lack of maturity
- Inability to demand respect
- Threat to the older and entrenched

Too old:

- Professionally demanding
- Slow to learn new techniques
- Lack of high-tech knowledge
- Older than management

Whatever the reason, you need to know how to counter those biases by creating a resume that will get you in the door for the interview and allow employers to evaluate you on a personal basis.

Most readers assume that your earliest listed employment began as soon as your education ended. Since most applicants from college graduate at 22, employers will assume you did too. If you feel you are too young, listing jobs you had while you were still in school can wipe the water from behind your ears. Choosing the functional form is also a good choice.

For those who fear they're too old, dropping your graduation date and some earlier positions from your resume will also seem to move up the starting date of your work history. The only thing you need to remember is that, from the date of your first listed position until the current time, all gaps in your employment history should be avoided.

If you are planning to drop earlier jobs to make yourself look younger, but still want to list some of those positions to reveal your wealth of experience, you can list those positions in a "Previous Experience" note at the end of your Work History. Avoid listing the years you held these jobs. Simply list the company name, your title, and the number of years you were employed in that position, as opposed to the actual dates you held the job.

Sample Resumes

CHAPTER 4

SANDRA'S READY FOR A POSITION AS A PRIVATE SCHOOL TEACHER

Sandra Pearson

Sandypear@ivillage.com
11 Hillhouse Aavenue
New Haven, Connecticut
06511
(203) 555-8103

Education:

Yale University, New Haven, CT
Bachelor of Arts, May 2002; Double Major
Psychology and History
1998 National Merit Scholar Award
1997 Micehouse National Laboratory Internship

Skills:

Microsoft Word, Word Perfect, Excel, ClarisWorks
Editing and proofreading
Proficient Spanish
Public Speaking
Design

Work Experience:

Project Hand in Hand 2002
Consultant to teach adults an accredited course on creating curriculum based on the Multiple Intelligence theory

Toddling On Up 1999-2002
Teacher, day care provider; creator of art curriculum and designer of weekly programs

Yale Greenpeace Office 2001
Distributed information on recycling, made presentations; visited, advised and reorganized locations in the Yale and New Haven Communities

Learning Disabilities Center at Yale 1999
Performed various clerical duties; read onto tapes and copied materials for special needs members of the Yale community

XYZ Vacuums
Sales representative for high-quality vacuum cleaners

Activities:

Kappa Betta Sorority 2000-2002; Social Chair 2001-2002
Community Relations Council 2000-2002
Black Alliance at Yale; Publicity Manager, 2000-2001
Yale Gospel Choir 1999-2002
Black Caucus at Yale; co-founder 2000-2002
Roots Theatre Ensemble; costume designer 1999-2000, actress 1999-2001
Yale Antigravity Society 2001

FARLEY CRAFTILY DISGUISES HIS GAPS IN WORK EXPERIENCE

Farley Suber

345 Fenwick Street Elton Park, CO 79403 (750) 555-4212

Objective: Seeking an entry-level position in sales or marketing

Education:
Bachelor of Arts in Communication (Public Relations) May 2002
Minor: Business/Liberal Arts
University of Chicago, Chicago, IL
Cumulative GPA: 3.1 out of 4.0

Experience:

LONS Computing Systems
Sales and Marketing Representative
- Applied marketing skills to increase sales of Macintosh computers
- Cultivated client relationships, increasing customer satisfaction and repeat sales
- Placed advertising in magazines including Men's Health, GQ, and Wired
- Wrote press releases on new computer products

Broadway Master Theatre
Marketing Assistant
- Assisted with the planning, creation and distribution of theatrical press releases
- Wrote radio advertisements
- Tracked attendance based on information from reservationists and box office attendants
- Handled photo releases mailings to be distributed to the media sources

Honors and Interests:

- **Senior Honors:** Senior cumulative average of 4.0 out of 4.0
- **Terrence S. Duboff Award:** Award for academic achievement excellence in communications
- **NCAA Division 1 Golfer:** Winner of the Greenview Collegiate Classic 2001, 2nd Place finalist 2001 NCAA MidWest Cup
- **Chi Phi Sigma Fraternity:** Rush Chairman, Scholarship Chairman, Standards Board, Senior Steering Committee

A GOOD ATTORNEY RESUME

BENITA APPELBEE
85-23 Jewel Ave.
Queens, New York 10128
(718) 454-8488
(718) 834-6216 fax
benitabomb@bom.com
www.bom.com/appelbee

PROFESSIONAL EXPERIENCE:
Eagle & Associates, Ltd., Yonkers, New York
Attorney, 2002-Present

- One of three attorneys law firm representing the United Car Rental Association in their landmark suit against Federal insurance regulation
- Monitored and analyzed legislation pertaining to the rental of motor vehicles, including:

Taxation	Registration	Water quality issues
Forfeiture	Environmental concerns	Employment
Impoundment	Solid waste	
Titling	Air quality	

- Designed and maintained the firm's web page and firm's peer-to-peer computer network

Hassel, Ebramsky & Brandwynn, New York, New York
Legal Assistant, 1998-1999

- Contributed to the team success of this 17-attorney law firm.
- Provided both legal and non-legal research and memorandum writing
- Assisted with litigation document production
- Monitored proposed legislation pertaining to environmental, insurance, health, transportation, taxation. and workers' compensation issues
- Responsible for marketing research of proposal for expanding the client base of the government relations department

1997 Vermont State Legislative Session, Albany, Vermont
Legislative Assistant, Spring 1997

- Monitored proposed legislation affecting the House Minority Caucus
- Conferred with state agencies, legislators, and lobbyists
- Wrote weekly bill summaries and status reports, drafted news releases and responded to letters from constituents

COMPUTER EXPERIENCE:
Research: Internet, Westlaw, Hoovers, and LexisNexis.
Software Proficiency: Word, WordPerfect, Excel, Access, and various office suite and internet applications including Netscape, Internet Explorer, Forte Agent, Eudora Pro, and Hotdog HTML editor.
Operating Systems: MS-Windows and MacOS X
Special Skills: HTML programming, WWW, Usenet, Gopher, and FTP. Some hardware experience, including managing a peer-to-peer network.

EDUCATION:
St. John's University School Of Law, Queens, NY
Degree: Juris Doctor, May 2002
Honors: Dean's List

St. Paul's University, St. Paul, MN
Degree: Double B.A. in History/Political Science and English, Magna Cum Laude, 1998
Honors:

- Phi Beta Kappa Honor Society
- President's Scholarship
- Dean's List
- College Fellow in History/Political Science
- Political Science Achievement Award

JOHN'S EXPERIENCE CAN BE CHRONOLOGICAL...

John Littles, Ph.D.

276 W. 87th Street #19H
New York, NY 10024
212-865-3118
e-mail: smalljohn@goal.net

SUMMARY OF QUALIFICATIONS

- Over 30 years directorial experience in mental health and developmental disabilities research and administration
- Experienced regional coordinator of community and state-operated programs
- Accomplished manager of annual budgets of more than $50 million

PROFESSIONAL EXPERIENCE

Program Consultant — **2002 — Present**
DisTechnological Company
Brooklyn, NY

- Applied three decades of healthcare knowledge to provide expert consultation
- Assisted a company's operations of residential and training programs for developmentally disabled residents
- Advised a high-tech company in developing the most efficient strategy for applying its technology to the health care industry

Chief Executive Officer — **1999 — 2002**
Mediseo, Brain Injury Rehabilitation Facility
New York, NY

- General oversight of brain rehabilitation treatment and research
- Supervised more than 100 medical and administrative staff
- Oversaw facility site relocation and expansion from a 300-bed to a 550-bed location

Facility Director/Regional Administrator — **1991 — 1999**
Deputy Director — **1983 — 1999**
New York State Department of Developmental Disabilities and Mental Health
Yonkers, NY

- Supervised 11 state-operated facilities as the director of this 500-bed mental health and developmental disabilities institution
- Supervised more than 50 community-based health care agencies

EDUCATION

BS, MS, PhD Biology 1977,1979,1983
Southeast Oklahoma State University
Shilo, Oklahoma

...OR FUNCTIONAL

John Littles, Ph.D.

276 W. 87th Street #19H
New York, NY 10024
212-865-3118
e-mail: smalljohn@goal.net

JOB OBJECTIVE

Director of Operations for a community based women's shelter

SUMMARY OF QUALIFICATIONS

- Over 30 years directorial experience in Mental Health and Developmental Disabilities research and administration
- Experienced regional coordinator of community and State operated programs
- Accomplished manager of annual budgets of over $50 million annually

PROFESSIONAL ACCOMPLISHMENTS

Directing
- Supervised 11 state-operated facilities as the director of New York State's third largest mental health facility for over 30 years
- Functioned as CEO of a brain injury rehabilitation and research facility
- Supervised 4 New York State facilities and over 50 community-based healthcare agencies
- Oversaw facility site relocation and expansion from a 300-bed to a 550-bed location
- Supervised 100 person medical and administrative staff

Consulting
- Applied three decades of health care knowledge to providing expert consultation
- Provided for a company that operated residential and training programs for developmentally disabled residents
- Advised a high-tech company in discovering the most efficient strategy for applying its technology to the health care industry

WORK EXPERIENCE

Program Consultant
DisTechnological Company, Brooklyn, NY — 2002-Present

Chief Executive Officer
Medisco, Brain Injury Facility, New York, NY — 1999-2002

Facility Director/Regional Administrator — 1991-1999
Deputy Director — 1983-1991
New York State Department of Developmental Disabilities and Mental Health Yonkers, NY

EDUCATION

BS, MS, PhD Biology 1977, 1979, 1983
Southeast Oklahoma State University
Shilo, Oklahoma

YVETTE'S TRYING TO REFOCUS HER CAREER ON MEDIA PR. THIS RESUME IS A GOOD START

Yvette Lindquist
3000 Tundra Circle
St. Paul, MN 44442
(606) 555-6622
yvette@clarity.net

OBJECTIVE
A broadcast public relations position.

EDUCATION

Viking Institute, Minneapolis, Minnesota
Course: Radio and Television Broadcasting
Certificate with Honors, July 2003
Academic Excellence Award

St. Viveca College, Minneapolis, Minnesota
Bachelor of Arts, May 1996
Major: Political Science. GPA: 3.4

EXPERIENCE

Broadcast News
Monitor, May 2002-present
• Monitored daily news broadcasts and logged information into national database
• Contacted clients regarding recent media coverage and provided radio and television
• Managed newsletters.

WMNO-TV
Viewer Services Representative, October 2001 to May 2002
Community Relations Representative, February 2000 to October 2001
• Responded to inquiries regarding news broadcasts and station activities.
• Coordinated Speaker Bureau, arranged talent public appearances and wrote speeches.
• Maintained Channel X Feedback arena on Internet.

Market Resource Associates
Public Relations Manager, May 1999 to February 2000
• Produced press releases, newsletters, advertisement layouts and media materials for home improvement companies.
• Coordinated "Supersaturated!" the first annual manufacturer and media reception at Eels R Us Aquarium.

Mink, Ferret & Otter Public Relations
Account Executive, November 1997 to March 1999
Assistant Account Executive, February 1997 to November 1997
Account Assistant, May 1996 to February 1997
• Wrote proposals.
• Developed budgets.
• Prepared news releases and media kits.
• Worked with journalists.
• Organized special promotion events.

NOTICE HOW GERRI BREAKS DOWN HER TECHNICAL SKILLS

Gerri Muniz
106 Convent Avenue, Apt. 18
Bronx, New York 10027
Home: (212) 281-0758
Pager: (917) 956-1764

OBJECTIVE

To obtain an entry-level position in database management.

WORK EXPERIENCE

City College, New York, NY
Academic Computing Department
September 2002 — Present
Technical Assistant

- Manage day-to-day computer support and networking problems within the computer lab
- Install and configure workstations
- Install various software applications on Windows workstations such as MS Office, Netscape, Dial-up Networking
- Troubleshoot basic LAN problems such as wiring and software clients
- Assist in the NetWare upgrade from Novell 5.1 to 6
- Assist in Novell backup procedures
- Assist in maintaining the school web site

Smart Fee Realty, New York, NY
July 2002 — September 2002
Administrative Assistant

- Oriented and instructed new clients and visitors
- Responsible for implementation of all office needs, supplies, and functions
- Handled realty materials
- Developed documents including homes listings and advertisements
- Organized documents, meetings, and open houses
- Composed documents for corporate office and all store locations, including spreadsheets and announcements

TECHNICAL SKILLS

Network:	MS Windows workstation. Novell 4.X server. Basic IPX, Basic TCP/IP, ThinNet, wiring. Upgrades, installations and configurations.
Software:	MS Office, ColdFusion Studio, Dreamweaver. Some knowledge of Adobe Photoshop, Paintshop Pro and Microsoft Image Composer
Hardware:	IBM compatibles for workstations and servers. Macintosh Computers
OS:	MS-DOS, basic knowledge of UNIX
Web Programs:	Well-versed in HTML, DHTML, JavaScript, VB Script, CGI and VRML

EDUCATION

Retts Electronic Institute, New York
Certificate: PC Technician

EILEEN USES DETAILED PROSE TO DESCRIBE HER BUSINESS ACHIEVEMENTS

EILEEN HONEY
323 East 13th Street Apt. 52
New York, New York 10003
(212) 555-9000
ehoney@futurenet.com

experience

FUTUREMED.COM, Inc., New York, NY — *2002-Present*
Principal and Founding Manager

Achievements:
- Designed company's premier online informational resource, featuring a live database, onsite search engine, and high-end content.
- Co-authored company's business plan.
- Assisted CFO in raising $500,000 in private equity.
- Launched marketing campaign to increase site advertiser participation from 10% to 50% of potential market.
- Managed sales campaign that resulted in 75% retention with on-site advertisers.
- Created system of virtual staff writers and editors from medical schools around the country.

Managerial Duties:
- Devise core business strategies including product development, marketing, sales, and promotion.
- Conduct in-person and telephone sales meetings with residency programs around the country.
- Train in-house telemarketing and sales staff.
- Coordinate promotional campaign to students and deans at the nation's 125 medical schools.
- Manage freelancers, virtual editors, and in-house sales and marketing staff.

HARVARD LAW SCHOOL, Cambridge, MA — *1999-2002*
Educational Technology Department, *Project Designer*

- Maintained Harvard's Interactive Video Library of educational CD-ROM titles.
- Monitored customer accounts, maintained client database, generated royalty reports.
- Handled marketing distribution to over 100 academic and corporate clients.
- Assisted in the writing and development of lesson guides, training manuals, and web page.
- Organized and attended biannual multimedia trade shows.
- Managed staff of 3-5 production assistants.

U.S. SUPREME COURT, Washington, D.C. — *1998-1999*

Honors Paralegal Program, *Paralegal Specialist*
- Criminal Division, Public Integrity Section
- Conducted legal research for active criminal cases.
- Organized and maintained pleadings and citizen inquiries.

Lands and Natural Resources Division, Policy, Legislation, and Special Litigation Section
- Monitored congressional activity related to environmental statutes.
- Handled requests for amicus curiae briefs.

Civil Rights Division, Employment Litigation Section
- Organized discovery materials for active sexual harassment cases.
- Conducted witness interviews for active race discrimination cases.

education

HARVARD UNIVERSITY, Cambridge, MA
A.B. in Psychology June 1999. GPA: 3.85/4.0. *Phi Beta Kappa*, Radcliffe Iota Chapter of Massachusetts.
Martha Stuart Smith Scholar. Elizabeth Cary Agassiz and John Harvard academic scholarships.

skills

Proficient in IBM and Apple Systems. Windows, MS Word, MS Excel, PowerPoint, FileMaker, Quark Xpress, HTML, extensive Internet industry knowledge.

GEORGIA HAS A LOT OF EXPERIENCE AND MANAGES TO PACK IT INTO A CLEARLY WRITTEN RESUME

Georgia Merrill
115 West 34th Street, Apt. 412 • New York, NY 10001 • 212-555-6378 • geowoman@hotmail.com

Experience

Quince Healthcare Properties Trust Santiago, Chile
Business Analyst January 2001-Present
The Quince Healthcare Properties Trust invests in high quality health and medical related properties in South America. Business Analyst responsibilities include:

- Execution of valuation analysis and financial due diligence for a $100 million bid for a Brazilian hospital group.
- Research of United States and South American hospital markets

Richardson Jamison LLC San Francisco, CA
Analyst — Mergers and Acquisitions July 1999-January 2001
Richardson Jamison LLC is an investment bank that provides strategic and analytical advice on mergers and acquisitions to a broad range of clients in the Information Technology industry. Areas of focus include Internet Content, Direct Marketing, Entertainment Software and Healthcare Information Systems. As an analyst, I:

- Performed financial analyses for development of client's acquisition strategy.
- Wrote five page profiles of potential acquisition targets exploring the company's products and services, sales and marketing, management and ownership and financial position.
- Primarily responsible for valuation and transaction analysis for $300 million sale of a public healthcare information systems company. Evaluated competitive offers, created presentation for seller's Board of Directors and executed detailed analysis of the transaction
- Contributed to Richardson's Strategic Marketing Program. Coordinated and edited article for Software Today, assisted in formulating questionnaire and analyzed results for the IT Forecast Report, wrote monthly press releases for the Richardson 100 Stock Index, and wrote a section of the 2000 Media M&A Report.

Yale in Washington Washington, D.C.
Coordinator April 1998-August 1998
Yale in Washington is the Yale University summer program for 100 students working in Washington, DC. Coordinator independently managed all aspects of the program including:

- Development of speaker series and recruitment of prominent figures, including Fawn Hall and George Bush, to address students on current issues and careers.
- Promotion of program to students through newsletter and organization of recreational costs.
- Production of final evaluation document which included recommendations to Yale Administration for future programs.

Education

Yale University New Haven, CT
Bachelor of Arts cum laude in American History, May 1999, GPA: 3.8/4.0
Honors: Dean's List (1997-1998), Pegasus Senior Honor Society (1% of class) and Phi Alpha Delta History Honor Society, Summa cum laude.
Activities: Served as President of the Whistle and Woof Society, a 600-member organization dedicated to campus service and community involvement. Directed all operations of a group including campus tours, recruitment and hosting of prospective students, tutoring, and community projects.
Other activities included Slumland Tutoring Project, College Peer Advising, Gamma Nu Gamma Sorority and attendance at Yale's Leadership Training Weekend.

Skills and Interests

Computer skills include Microsoft Office — Excel, Word, and PowerPoint. Community Service through Street Project, New York including volunteering with a 6th grade class from Bayard Elementary School and at the University Soup Kitchen, Extensive travel in Central and South America. Fluent in Spanish.

GORDON'S AMASSED AN EXCELLENT RECORD IN SALES WITHIN ONE JOB THAT MERITS A BREAKDOWN OF RESPONSIBILITIES

GORDON PRIZZI
276 W. 188 St. Apt.9B
New York, NY 10044
212-726-9788

education

Class of 2002 **UNIVERSITY OF MARYLAND** **COLLEGE PARK, MD**
Bachelor of Arts in Sociology. Activities: The Greek Task Force; Senior Class Steering Committee; Senior Class Gift Drive; The Terrapin Fund; Groundhog Society; Intramural Water Polo. Awarded: Alpha Oli, Greek (Fraternity/Sorority) National Honor Society, inducted Spring 1994

experience **MACY'S** **NEW YORK, NY**

9/2003 — Present *Senior Assistant Buyer, Macy's Ladies Shoes*. Responsibilities:
- Source new vendors for innovative shoe styles
- Negotiate with 12 store general managers for prime main floor locations
- Participate in all stages of product development for over 75 different commodities
- Work with the Stroll Group (licensing agent) and Group 9 Design (marketing and design agency) on licensing logistics and negotiating royalty fees with vendors
- Develop and execute full-fledged marketing campaign and $300,000 financial plan for new shop launch

5/03 — 9/03 *Senior Assistant Buyer, Lingerie*. Responsibilities in addition to all previous Assistant Buyer Responsibilities:
- Negotiated advertising funding allowances for focal department
- Developed and executed six month seasonal marketing and financial plans for focal department
- Had accountability for all financial elements at end of season, including: store sales, markdowns, purchases, stock level, gross margin percent, and gross margin dollars
- Trained and oversaw one Assistant Buyer in all aspects of former position
- Oversaw and prioritized two group assistants

9/02 — 5/03 *Assistant Buyer, Lingerie*. Responsibilities:
- Viewed new lines and participated in choice of product
- Placed, maintained, and expedited orders for twenty store locations
- Coordinated all activities between the central buying office, vendors, and department managers
- Wrote advertising copy and acquired merchandise samples for newspaper and catalogue advertising shoots
- Synthesized store activity data to create periodic recap reports
- Determined merchandise for point-of-sale and hard-line mark-downs
- Negotiated and executed Returns to Vendor (RTV)

Summer 2002 **SLOW BANK** **BOSTON, MA**
- Intern, *Poky Review*, internal bank magazine. Responsibilities:
- Researched long-term labor trends, utilizing computers, periodical literature, and interviews
- Analyzed and synthesized trend data, while composing and editing "My Turn" column

Summer 2001 **THE EMERALD COMPANY** **NEW YORK, NY**
- Intern, Investment Management and Trust Company. Responsibilities:
- Researched and prepared corporate profiles for use by external investors
- Analyzed corporate annual reports to determine foreign sales and earnings percentages

additional

2/1999-5/2002 **BETA BETA PI FRATERNITY** **COLLEGE PARK, MD**

12/00-12/01 *President*. Prepared agendas for and conducted Chapter meetings; Represented Chapter to the President's Roundtable for discussion of University issues; Attended National Foundation Leadership Training School

12/99-12/00 *Treasurer*. Prepared annual $150,000 budget; Billed and collected dues, fee, and rents from 135 chapter members; Processed 50 accounts payable per month; Prepared financial statements for auditor

personal Proficient in Chinese. Interests include cologne, golf, and volunteer work for Princess Diana memorial Foundation.

COVER LETTERS

Overview

Often, people look at the cover letter as an afterthought in the application process, a mere formality. Dangerous thinking.

The cover letter is your first chance to have a conversation with your prospective employer, to tell them who you are, why you're contacting them, and to explain away any inconsistencies or peculiarities about your resume. It's a brief, one-sided conversation, of course, but one you should enter.

Because your cover letter serves as a fuller expression of your personality, it is, in a sense, more important than your resume. While employers want employees with the skills to fit the job, candidates who can put together words, and express themselves in a clear, appealing manner, are favored by any future boss.

While creating a good cover letter can be an elusive task, creating a bad cover letter that will trash your employment chances is surprisingly easy. Like resumes, many applicants instantly lose legitimacy because of careless typos or oddball inclusions.

Because cover letters require more subjective writing, there's more that can go wrong. The cover letter demands that you display your command of the language, your grammatical expertise and your social grace. Only through study and practice can you ensure success.

Be Prepared

CHAPTER 5

"The general who loses a battle makes but few calculations beforehand. Thus do many calculations lead to victory, and few calculations to defeat."

The Art of War
Sun Tzu
5th Century B.C.

It's not enough to glance at an ad and start writing your cover letter. You've got to make sure the letter looks right, and that it doesn't sound like you've sent the very same one to three hundred other employers that weekend. Tailoring your letter specifically to the company and the position will impress recruiters and give you an added edge. Here are the techniques that will let you get all the info you can about a company without resorting to high-priced surveillance equipment.

Company web sites

The explosion of the web as a medium of business communication has made getting basic information about companies easier and faster. Many companies now have web sites on which they either conduct business or advertise their business to potential internet clients. These sites are excellent sources of information on a company's history, new products or services, size, sales revenue and locations.

Web searching

Running a company name through web browsers such as Yahoo!, or Google can quickly pull information on a specific company. Also, sites such as Vault and Hoovers specialize in company information. Finally, you should take a look at the company's web site, if they have one. Another avenue of insider information: message boards. Try the company-specific message boards on Vault or Yahoo! to connect with current and former employees or other job seekers.

LexisNexis

One of the most effective ways to get information on a company is through a LexisNexis search. The immensely powerful and exceedingly expensive LexisNexis database lets you access nearly every article published on your subject. LexisNexis is updated daily with newspaper and magazine articles from around the country.

While personal access is possible, the cost is heavy, based on each search you do, which limits the amount of experimenting you can do to find the documents you need. Those willing to pay the price can set up an account at LexisNexis Express, http://www.lexis.com/xchange/. Individuals can also arrange to have LexisNexis researchers perform the search to maximize results.

Vault employer profiles and surveys

Coincidentally, the folks at Vault, the fine institution that brought you this very book, spend a great deal of time doing in-depth research on top employers. If you're looking for info on a major employer, Vault offers three- to 60-page reports on a company's history, plans for the future, workplace culture and hiring practices. On the Vault web site, you can also read employee surveys for hundreds of top employers. To research companies on Vault, go to www.vault.com.

HERE'S A GREAT EXAMPLE OF RESEARCH LEADING TO AN OUTSTANDING COVER LETTER

Thom Flanton
Hiring Manager
Merck and Biddle
40 Wall Street
New York, NY 10001
(212) 349-4198

August 19, 2003

Dear Mr. Flanton,

I recently graduated with my Associates Degree in Accounting and Financial Planning looking for a full position in the bookkeeping field and I am extremely interested in beginning my career at Merck and Biddle. The investing history of Merck and Biddle was the subject of my final undergraduate thesis, its stability in the junk bond heavy 1980's, its rise to strength and this its consequent prominence in the 1990's.

I feel I have much to offer M & B's drive toward involving a younger generation of investors. As the founder of the Oberlin Students Investment Group, I managed the capital of 31 of my peers, making 9% annual return over a three year period, all the while maintaining a 3.8 average in my field. I want to apply that vision and multitasking ability at Merck and Biddle.

Merck and Biddle is my first choice for my entry into the professional arena, and I believe that my employment would be highly beneficial to Merck and Biddle as well. As co-Founder Charles Anderson said in his 1962 commencement speech at Brown University, "There is no more sound investment than youth."

Thank you very much for your time and consideration, I look forward to discussing with you the ways I can contribute to Merck and Biddle's future.

Sincerely,

Marisa Benson

The Cover Letter Template

CHAPTER 6

WONDERING WHAT GOES ON A COVER LETTER? HERE'S A STEP-BY-STEP GUIDE

Your Name
Your Street Address, Apartment #
Your City, State Zip
Your Email Address
Your (h) PHONE NUMBER
Your (f) FAX NUMBER

Contact's Name
Contact's Title
Contact's Department
Contact's Name
Contact's Street Address, Suite #
Company City, State Zip
Company PHONE NUMBER
Company FAX NUMBER

Date

Dear Ms./Mr. CONTACT,

The first paragraph tells why you're contacting the person, then either mentions your connection with that person or tells where you read about the job. It also quickly states who you are. Next it wows them with your sincere, researched knowledge of their company. The goal: demonstrating that you are a worthy applicant, and enticing them to read further.

The second and optional third paragraph tell more about yourself, particularly why you're an ideal match for the job by summarizing why you're what they're looking for. You may also clarify anything unclear on your resume.

The last paragraph is your goodbye: you thank the reader for his or her time. Include that you look forward to their reply or give them a time when you'll be getting in contact by phone.

Sincerely,

Sign Here

Date

Placement of the date, whether left justified, centered or aligned to the right, is up to your discretion, but take the time to write out the entry. If you choose to list the day, list it first, followed by the month, date, and year, as follows: Tuesday, July 9, 2003. (Europeans commonly list the day before month, so writing a date only in numbers can be confusing. Does a letter written on 4/7/04 date from April 7, or July 4?)

Name and address

Your name and address on the cover letter should be the same as the one on your resume. Uniformity in this case applies not only to the address given, but the way the information is written. If you listed your street as Ave. instead of Avenue on your resume, do so on your cover letter too.

Your header can be displayed centrally, just like the resume header — including your name in a larger and/or bolded font. But in most cases, the heading is either left justified or left justified and indented to the far right hand side of the page.

If you choose to list your phone number, make sure that you don't list it somewhere else on the page.

Next comes the address of the person you are writing. In many circumstances, you'll have the complete information on the person you're trying to contact, in which case you should list it in this order:

- Name of contact
- Title of contact
- Company name
- Company address
- Phone number
- Fax number

However, in many cases, you have less than complete information to go on. This is particularly true when responding to an advertisement. If you have an address or phone or fax number but no company name, try a reverse directory, such as the online GTE Superpages (http://superpages.gte.net/), which lets you trace a business by either its address or phone number.

When you're trying to get a name of a contact person, calling the company and asking the receptionist for the name of the recipient (normally, though not always, head of HR) may work. But usually, companies don't list this information because they don't want you calling at all. So if you call, be polite, be persistent, ask for a contact name, say thank you and hang up. Don't identify yourself. If you have questions, wait until the interview.

If you don't get all of the info, don't worry. There are several salutations to use to finesse the fact that you've got no idea who you're addressing. Some solutions are:

To whom it may concern: A bit frosty, but effective.

Dear Sir or Madam: Formal and fusty, but it works.

Sirs: Since the workforce is full of women, avoid this outdated greeting.

Omitting the salutation altogether: Effective, but may look too informal.

Good morning: A sensible approach that is gaining popularity.

Format

Unlike the resume, the cover letter offers the writer significant room for flexibility. Successful cover letters have come in various different forms, and sometimes cover letters that break rules achieve success by attracting attention. But most don't. Here are some basic guidelines on what information the body of a cover letter should deliver.

First paragraph

To be successful, this first paragraph should contain:

- A first line that tells the reader why you're contacting them, and how you came to know about the position. This statement should be quick, simple and catchy. Ultimately, what you're trying to create is a descriptive line by which people can categorize you. This means no transcendental speeches about "the real you" or long-winded treatises on your career and philosophy of life.
- Text indicating your respect for the firm's accomplishments, history, status, products, or leaders.
- A last line that gives a very brief synopsis of who you are and why you want the position. The best way to do this, if you don't already have a more personal connection with the person you're contacting, is to lay it out like this:

I am a (your identifying characteristic)

+

I am a (your profession)

+

I have (your years of experience or education)

+

I have worked in (your area of expertise)

+

I am interested in (what position you're looking for)

And thus a killer first paragraph is born.

Middle paragraph(s)

The middle paragraph allows you to move beyond your initial declarative sentences, and into more expansive and revealing statements about who you are and what skills you bring to the job. This is another opportunity to explicitly summarize key facts of your job history. The middle paragraph also offers you the opportunity to mention any connection or prior experience that you may have with the company.

Tell the employer in this paragraph how, based on concrete references to your previous performances, you will perform in your desired position. This does not mean making general, unqualified statements about your greatness such as "I'm going to be the best you've ever had" or my "My energetic multi-tasking will be the ultimate asset to your company."

Comments should be backed up by specific references. Try something along the lines of "My post-graduate degree in marketing, combined with my four years of retail bicycle sales would make me a strong addition to Gwinn Cycles' marketing team."

Or: "Meeting the demands of a full-time undergraduate education, a position as student government accountant, and a 20-hour-a-week internship with Davidson Management provided me with the multi-tasking experience needed to excel as a financial analyst at Whittier Finance."

Many advertisements ask you to name your salary requirements. Some avoid the problem altogether by ignoring this requirement, and this may be the safest route — any number you give might price you out of a job (before you have the chance to negotiate face-to-face at an interview). Alternatively, you might be pegged at a lower salary than you might otherwise have been offered. If you must give a salary requirement, be as general as possible The safest bet is to offer as general a range as possible ("in the $30,000s"). Put the salary requirement at the end of the paragraph, not in your first sentence.

Some cover letter writers use another paragraph to describe their accomplishments. This makes sense if, for example, your experience lies in two distinct areas, or you need to explain something that is not evident on your resume, such as "I decided to leave law school to pursue an exciting venture capital opportunity" or "I plan to relocate to Wisconsin shortly." Do not get overly personal — "I dropped out of business school to care for my sick mother" is touching, but will not necessarily impress employers.

Final paragraph

The final paragraph is your fond farewell, your summation, a testament to your elegance and social grace. This should be the shortest paragraph of the letter. Here, tell your readers you're pleased they got so far down the page. Tell them you look forward to hearing from them. Tell them how you can be reached. Here's some sample sentences for your conclusion.

Thank you sentences:

Thank you for your time.

Thank you for reviewing my qualifications.

Thank you for your consideration.

Thank you for your review of my qualifications.

Way too much:

It would be more than an honor to meet with you.

A note of confidence in a callback:

I look forward to your reply.

I look forward to hearing from you.

I look forward to your response.

I look forward to your call.

Over the top:

Call me tomorrow, please.

THE FOLLOWING TWO WRITERS MADE SURE THEIR COVER LETTERS INCLUDED ALL OF THE REQUIRED ELEMENTS IN AN APPROPRIATE PLACE

October 1, 2003

Martin Kalinsky
434 Tech. Rd.
Boston, MA. 24536
232-555-9999

Hugh Brock
Director, Theoretical Physics Institute
343 Accelerator Lane
Baltimore, MD. 76594

Dear Mr. Brock,

In researching ways in which people have made their marks in the field of physics, I cannot tell you how many times I have encountered your name in journals, newspaper articles, and textbooks. Your contribution has been truly stunning.

Now that I find myself in the position of seeking my own fate in the field, I wanted to ask if you could offer fifteen minutes of your time to discuss ways in which a neophyte such as myself can best forge a path of his own. I am a senior at M.I.T. specializing in the Acceleration Norms of Random Ratio Quantum Particles.

I will follow this letter with a call to the Institute to see if I can schedule an appointment. It would be an honor to speak to you.

Very truly yours,

Martin Kalinsky

RALPH MAKES A CONVINCING CASE FOR HIMSELF

August 3, 2003

David Pomme de Terre
Sales Manager
Maine Potato Council
333 Remington Lane So.
Tuber, Maine

Ralph G. Getter
555 Grogan Ave. #2
Portland, MN
325-555-4444
rgett@sales.net

Dear David:

This letter is to apply to the opening in Sales at the Maine Potato Council.

Maine potatoes are in my blood. My father George was a farmer near Bangor, and I used to help him harvest them and take them into market. Unfortunately, my father was forced to sell the farm — another loss to the competition from Idaho. Seeing the farm go under has increased my strong belief that Maine potato needs the help of lobbying councils like your organization. If the enclosed resume states the barest of facts about my educational background and experiences, let this letter state my passion for Maine potatoes and all they stand for.

I hope that you will consider inviting me in for an interview to discuss the position. Thank you for your time and consideration. I look forward to hearing from you soon.

Sincerely,

Ralph G. Getter

Types of Cover Letters

CHAPTER 7

Job listing cover letters

The most common way to hunt for jobs is to check newspaper and online listings. For many, the first step in any job search is opening up the Sunday paper and seeing who is hiring, how much they are paying, and what experience they demand. Some prefer to browse job search sites, while others go directly to the company web site. The effectiveness of responding to these ads is debatable. Often, companies list openings only because of "open door" regulations and have already chosen an internal candidate. Many openings are filled through connections before the first letters come in. Still other ads are placed by companies or recruitment agencies, which simply wish to test the waters. Even if the ad is legitimate, it is sure to attract dozens, even hundreds of other applicants. That's why having a stand-out cover letter is vital.

When responding to an advertised position, explain that fact in the first sentence. List the exact name of the advertised job title, the name of the newspaper the ad was in and the day and date the ad ran. Because companies often run several different ads at once, or ads for more than one position within a department, writing "I'm responding to the advertised sales position" may not be enough.

RALEIGH RESPONDS TO AN ADVERTISEMENT

October 1, 2003

Raleigh Collins
78 Juniper Lane
Fairview, NC 24523?

Art Director
Polymer Productions
Fax (817) 482-9025

Dear Sir or Madam:

I am writing in response to your advertisement in the *Columbia Journal Classifieds* for a copywriter. I am a copywriter with 8 years experience conceptualizing and producing engaging copy for catalogs, annual reports, brochures and all types of collateral material. In addition, my writing abilities have helped me create original works of art for clients like Mead Coated Papers and Oxford Healthcare. I am well-versed in MS Word and WordPerfect, as well as both Macintosh and PC platforms.

Much of my work has been crafted for the following clients; Macmillan Reference Library, Watson Guptill Publications, Mead Coated Papers, Cambridge Healthcare, W.W. Norton, Hawaii University Press, and *Arcade Fashion & Lifestyle Magazine.*

I have confidence in my ability to produce powerful, gripping copy for your organization. My experience allows me to complete any project from concept to the final stages at a fast pace to meet deadlines, and to package it for the Web.

I look forward to hearing from you. Thank you for your time and consideration.

Yours sincerely,

Raleigh Collins

ROB MAKES HIS INTEREST CLEAR

Rob Sexton
94 Hopalong Street
Alexandria, MI 20006
Robse23@aol.com
(904) 555-0009

Staffing, Job Code: OXP-CRGB95
Amgen Center
Thousands Oaks, CA 91320-1789
(805) 447-1000
(805) 499-9981 (fax)

Dear Sir/Madam:

Enclosed please find my resume, which I am sending in response to your advertisement for the position of research associate. In the 15 years since the introduction of Epogen, Amgen has proven that while it knows how to find success in the present, its greatest concern is the future. I want to contribute towards that future.

Over the last three years, my interest in the application of chemical innovations to human problems has helped me sustain my full schedule. I graduated in May 2000 from St. John's University with a bachelor of science degree majoring in Chemical Engineering. As you will see from my resume, in addition to meeting the demands of a full-time academic schedule and achieving a 3.6 cumulative overall average and a 4.0 average in the last two years of my major, I have also accrued two years of experience in commercial chemical research. In both school and work, I have worked closely with teams of chemists and bioengineers.

My experience, along with the enthusiasm and high energy I will bring to the job, qualifies me for the position you are seeking to fill. I have included my transcript and references as supplements to my resume. I hope they demonstrate what I can offer to Amgen. I look forward to the opportunity of meeting you for an interview. Thank you very much for your time and any consideration you may give me.

Sincerely,

Rob Sexton

BRET USES COMPANY RESEARCH TO COMPOSE A GREAT COVER LETTER

October 1, 2003

Bret Orfman
329 San Opp Ave.
San Francisco, CA 80808
203-323-9986

Lucille Craft
Account Director
Joyhut Advertising
1 Madison Avenue
NY, NY 10005

Dear Lucille:

I would like to express my interest in Joyhut Advertising and the available Account Executive position described on your agency's web site.

After four years at Stanford University, where I majored in English and wrote for the school paper, I leapt into the competitive world of advertising at Olf and Oleman Worldwide in San Francisco. For the past year, I have served a valuable apprenticeship in the advertising industry, working as an assistant account executive on the Harbinger Sporting Goods account.

During my time on the Harbinger account, the company's advertising spending has increased by two million dollars, and I have progressed from having very little client contact to interfacing with the client-side on a regular basis. Since my introduction to the world of advertising, it has been my goal to work on Madison Avenue.

I would very much like to discuss the open position. Thank you for your time spent reading this letter and the enclosed resume. I look forward to hearing from you soon.

Sincerely,

Bret Orfman

Networking cover letters

Friends, acquaintances and family may sometimes tip you off to openings or currently hiring employers. This necessitates a different approach to the cover letter — the schmoozing cover letter.

Connections are beautiful, fragile things that need to be cultivated, so make sure you follow the proper networking etiquette. Do not use networking cover letters to ask for a job. People with the power to hire new employees take their responsibilities as gatekeepers seriously, and some stranger asking for a job only turns a gatekeeper off. But networking cover letters asking for career advice, information on the industry or just more contacts can often convince a powerful person like a hiring manager to become a more welcoming mentor.

Furthermore, employment leads usually don't appreciate cold calls. Instead of "When can you come in for an interview," the question you'll most likely hear is "Where exactly did you get my number from?" Even when your mutual acquaintance alerts them that you are calling, a cold call can still be ineffective because contacts have no concrete idea of your experience, skill level, or ability to function in the professional world. With no idea of who you really are, how do you expect them to help you?

Providing contacts with a killer cover letter and resume lets them have everything they need to know about you. And by the time you call, they can be prepared to tell you where you do or if you don't fit into their hiring plan. Depending on how strong the contacts are, they might also be able to give you insider information on how you can make your cover letter and resume even more effective for the company in question.

Here are some tips to ensure your networking cover letter has what it takes.

- State simply and clearly in the first paragraph exactly what you're looking for, and what it is that you want from your contact. But remember, you're investigating opportunities, not begging for a job. Since few people have the power to hand out jobs on the spot, there's no point in asking.
- Focus your area of professional interest without being limiting. Avoid overly broad sentences such as "I'm looking for a position in sales, or as a lab assistant, or as the night watchman or janitor." On the other hand, listing an exact position, such as "Associate Marketing Director," limits your inquiry to one position and increases the chances of a negative response. The best way to walk this thin line is to state the level (senior, entry-level, mid-level) of the position followed by the field you are interested in.
- Mention in the last line that you will be in contact. Making contact is your responsibility, so don't meekly wait to be called. To avoid calling at a bad time, try the morning or when you know your contact will be out but a receptionist will be in. Ask the receptionist for the best time to call. Once you get your contact on the line, ask if the present is a good time to talk or if you should set up another phone appointment when it's more convenient.

- Send the cover letter and resume to the individual's work address, even if you have a home address. If you don't know the contact's business address, call the company and get it, along with the contact title and department.

CHECK OUT THE FOLLOWING LETTERS – EXCELLENT SCHMOOZING VIA THE POST OFFICE

291 N. Cuda Street Apt. 5G
Shanto, KY 42788
July 23, 2004

Jane Parson
Marsha Belini and Associates
552 Highland Avenue, Suite 800
Millersville, KY 42781

Dear Jane:

Thank you for your time on the telephone this morning. Per our conversation, I am writing to express an interest in a Business Development position with Belini and Associates. I received my BA in Psychology from Billings in 1994 and am currently a Principal and Manager at Marketdriven.com, Inc., a venture-backed growth-stage Internet company.

I have nearly four years of experience working in a small business/entrepreneurial setting. My most recent experience with Marketdriven.com, an online career-planning web site for marketing students and professionals, has allowed me to participate hands-on in all facets of an expanding business, including product development, marketing, sales, and promotion. During my first three months with the company, I worked closely with a web development firm to design the content and features of the site, which include a dynamic database, passwords for advertisers, an on-site search engine, and high-end content.

At the same time, I was writing the company's business plan, which is currently being used to raise $1,000,000 in equity financing. I also devised a unique format for the site's advertiser participation from 17 percent to 37 percent of the potential market. In addition, I created a network of virtual writers and editors from medical schools around the country who actively contribute to the site's content.

I believe that my writing, collaboration, and presentation skills are excellent, and I am committed to creativity and excellence in new media business development. I am interested in working in a fast-paced, team-oriented environment where I could make a significant contribution to a growing Internet business.

I have enclosed my resume for your review. I look forward to hearing from you. Thank you for your time.

Regards,

Wendy Boyd

COLETTE CITES A CONNECTION IN HER COVER LETTER

May 15, 2004

Eric Chong
Head of Production
As the Paint Dries
Fox Television
676 Sunset Blvd. Rm. 303
Los Angeles, CA. 88433

Dear Eric:

Caroline George informed me that you might be looking for someone to fill the production assistant position on the set of *As the Paint Dries*.

Caroline witnessed my work on *UCLA Blues*, a soap opera filmed and broadcast on the UCLA campus. Caroline was the mentor of the program and encouraged my pursuit of production work beyond college. I feel that my experience on the set of *UCLA Blues* and my degree in Film have given me the necessary background to immediately function as a valuable member of the *As the Paint Dries* team.

I have enclosed my resume for your review. I will try to contact you within the week to arrange an interview. Thank you for your time and consideration.

Sincerely,

Colette McInnis

Cold mailing

Cold mailings are the toughest entries into a company. The recipients don't know you, don't know anyone who knows you, and certainly didn't ask you to contact them. But cold mailings do have one advantage: they show your initiative and genuine interest in a company.

The effectiveness of cold mailings ultimately depends upon the establishment you contact. Some well-organized companies actually keep resumes on file and pull them when they begin hiring. But before you rush to mail letters to every Fortune 500 company, understand that most companies lack the organization to take such care with your resume. The onus is on you.

You need to demonstrate your interest in a company by presenting your knowledge about that company's history, current projects, and business plan. Once you know its plan for the future, you can tell the company how you will contribute to that strategy. (Roll out our research section for information on investigative tactics.)

Make sure you're addressing an individual. Call reception and ask for the head of the department in which you're interested. Hiring decisions are made by the people within the department, not Human Resources, so if you have a choice, avoid HR. Contacting an individual can also create a feeling of personal responsibility in the reader that might save your documents from the shredder. Seeing one's own name creates a sense of accountability that an anonymous posting doesn't inspire.

VIRGINIA DOES HER RESEARCH AND FINDS AN HR CONTACT

March 19, 2004

Maureen Johnson
222 Rally Road
Lafayette, LA. 77474
415-756-7771
mojo@usl.edu

Gordon Thane
Director of Human Resources
Bureaucracy International
555 Executive Row
New York, NY 10203

Dear Mr. Thane:

This letter is to inquire into the availability of administrative positions in Customer Services for Bureaucracy International, a company I have long admired and with which I would like to be associated.

In anticipation of my graduation from the University of Southwest Louisiana in May, I am exploring possibilities in customer service. For the past five years, I have refined my interpersonal skills working as a waitress at Pere Jimmy's Restaurant in downtown Lafayette, where I have risen to the rank of assistant manager and consistently worked very hard to please our demanding customers.

I am interested in customer services because I have found I get an incredible satisfaction from solving problems. My work at Pere Jimmy's and my experience soliciting university contributions over the phone have prepared me to become a successful member of your team.

My resume is enclosed for your review. I will call within the week to make sure you have received it and to inquire about the possibility of setting up an interview. Thanks for your time and consideration.

Sincerely,

Virginia Johnson

Interoffice cover letter

Those who find themselves in offices of imposing size and multi-acre parking lots may find that in-house job openings occasionally demand cover letters. When sending an interoffice cover letter, don't be lulled by the fact that you and the reader share a health care plan.

Remember, the cover letter is a structured document, and that structure needs to be respected for the reader to respect your application. The header should be the same as a regular cover letter but for one detail: the address. Aside from the company name, don't bother putting information that you and the reader share.

WILLIAM FOLLOWS COVER LETTER ETIQUETTE TO A T

William Baxson
Electric Engineer
Showcase Arena
Ext. 8851

April 6, 2004

Mr. Pete Carlton
Senior Site Manager
Showcase Arena
Ext. 8830

Dear Mr. Carlton,

I found your request for a Level IV Electrical Site Manager among the Showcase Interoffice memo board; it sounded very interesting to me. I currently work for Bill Wilkins in the Events Planning Division, and, as he will be retiring this Fall, I have been looking for a position in Site Management to apply my skills and 22 years of engineering and management experience.

I'm very organized, I'm a self-motivated worker, but I enjoy working as a team player. My belief is that since we spend the majority of our lives in the workplace, work should be a pleasant experience. As a manager, I try to make the job one that employees enjoy going to everyday. Not only has this kept those under my supervision satisfied, it has enabled me to run the most efficient workgroups at Tri Edison. I would like to continue my success under your direction in Site Management.

If my experience and management philosophy are attractive to you, please feel free to contact me at the Events Planning office or beeper number 7309. Thank you for your consideration.

Very truly yours,

William Baxson

E-mailing cover letters

Something happens to people when they get online. Maybe it's the instant access, maybe it's the "I-could-be-naked" anonymity, but when people get online they sometimes get overly casual and informal. This might be fine when your talking to your buddy in Omaha or the sweetheart you just met in a chatroom, but it doesn't work well when you're trying to get business done.

Just because you're communicating online does not mean you should consider yourself exempt from any of the formalities of paper-based communication. Online cover letters are notoriously awful, poorly written throwaways of fewer than three lines whose only purpose is to say "I'm applying, this is my resume, have a nice day."

When formatting the cover letter, stick to left-justified headers and four-inch wide text lines in your paragraphs. You never know when the address you're mailing to has a small e-mail-page format that will awkwardly wrap text around the screen. Also, many e-mail systems cannot handle text enhancements like bolding, bulleting or underlining, so play it safe by using CAPITAL LETTERS — or dashes — if you need to make an emphasis.

Proper E-mail Cover Letter Etiquette

Anil Dash, the former chief information technology officer for an online music video production studio in Manhattan, lost his job this January when the company fired nearly all its employees. Since then, Dash figures he's applied for more than a dozen jobs, contacting every one of the potential employers - befitting an out-of-work CIO - through e-mail.

But every time he prepares another e-mail, he faces a choice. Should he bother to write an e-mail cover letter, the sort of thing he'd do if he were mailing the resume, or should he merely dash off a few lines to the effect of, "Hi, I'm interested in your job, and I've attached my resume as a Word file. Thanks."

"I do cover letters for jobs I really want," Dash says. "For ones I don't care about, I just spam them."

Why cover letters still matter

According to recruiting experts, Dash is doing the right thing by writing extensive e-mail cover letters. Even though cover letters came of age in the age of pen and paper (or typewriter and paper), they still have a place in the 21st century, when want ads, resumes, and interviews all fly over virtual networks.

"It's going over the Internet, but it's the same product," Madeline Miller, the manager of Compu-Type Nationwide Resume Service in upstate New York, said of e-mail cover letters. "The cover is very important and it should be the same quality if you were to mail it."

Since e-mail messages generally tend to be conversational and quickly written, many people aren't used to drafting carefully written e-mail cover letters. But Miller said any applicant who creates a fully-fleshed e-mailed cover letter has an advantage over an applicant with a more slapdash cover letter.

"There is a tendency to jot off a few lines, and people might write, "I'm applying for this job, here is my resume," Miller said. "But if there is a cover letter, that could put somebody over the top."

But at the same time, make sure your e-mailed cover letter isn't a chore to read. If brevity is a virtue with conventional cover letters, it's a necessity for e-mailed cover letters.

Appropriate cover letter length

Reesa Staten, the research director for OfficeTeam, a staffing service firm, says e-mailed cover letters shouldn't run more than two or three paragraphs.

"You want to include the same type of information, albeit in a shorter version," Staten said. "What you don't want to do is rehash your resume. There's no need to restate what you've done in the past. What you want to do is tell them where you learned about the listing, why you're right for the job, and how they can reach you."

Tips for sending cover letters and resumes

If you really want the job, follow up an e-mailed cover letter and resume with a hard copy you mail. Make sure this hard copy includes a cover letter, too, that restates who you are and why you're qualified. Somewhere in the cover letter, be sure to write, "I recently e-mailed you my resume and I'm following up with this hard copy."

Why should you do this? A hard copy gives your resume another chance for exposure and makes it easier for a potential boss to pass around or file your cover letter and resume. In cases where your e-mailed cover letter and resume have been overlooked in someone's in-box or rendered inaccessible by a computer glitch, a hard copy may be your only chance for exposure.

If you're including a resume as an attachment, first make sure the prospective employer accepts attachments. Then, in your cover letter, mention the program you used to create your attachment. ("I've enclosed a cover letter written in Microsoft Word 2000.") It's also a good idea to include a cut and paste text version of your resume in addition, in case the person reading the resume doesn't have the software to open your attachment.

With any resume file you're attaching, open it first to make sure it's updated, error free, and the version of your resume you want to send. Sending a virus is tantamount to sealing your job-doom.

Save a copy of whatever you send by including your own e-mail address in the "BCC" field or by making sure a copy goes to your "Sent mail" folder. This allows you to resend the letter if a problem pops up.

Lastly, don't fill in the "to" field with the recipient's e-mail address until you've finished writing and editing the cover letter and resume. This prevents you from accidentally sending off the message before it's ready.

Networking thanks

Regardless of the outcome of your job search, you want to send a thank you letter to the contact who got you in the door in the first place. Contacts need to be maintained, and even if things didn't go as hoped this time, that doesn't mean that next time they won't. If you treat the contact properly, they'll be more inclined to keep their ear to the ground for future openings they may hear about.

Even if a contact is one of your best friends, don't take him or her for granted. We all have lots of friends, but how many would you recommend to come work at your place of business? A professional note is not only considerate, it shows that you can handle yourself gracefully in a business setting.

Avoid! Cover Letter Errors

CHAPTER 8

Oops!

Despite the fact that companies consistently demand that applicants submit cover letters along with their resumes, many job seekers still believe the cover letter to be nothing but a mild formality. Sometimes they don't bother sending a cover letter at all or just one paragraph notes, quickly belted out with little thought.

When you send a poor cover letter, you send the message that you can't get the job done, even when quality is essential. Unless you enjoy sitting around in the house ducking calls from bill collectors, that's not the kind of message you want to send.

Too short is too bad

Many people send one paragraph, two- or three-sentence throwaway notes in place of real cover letters. Or they confuse the cover letter with a dashed-off note, such as the fax coversheet. A cover letter should have three to four paragraphs, no paragraphs of over six lines long, with the longest one being the middle one or two, and the shortest one being the final, summation paragraph. The idea is to make the document brief and easily readable while still demonstrating a professional, thoughtful manner.

A COVER LETTER THAT DOESN'T MEET THE COVER LETTER LENGTH STANDARD

Ms. Camachi,

I am very interested in the position you have advertised and would very much enjoy woking at Minton Advertising. Although I am only available for the summer, I hope that you can review my resume and that it might be possible for me to work at Minton this summer. Thank you for your consideration.

Catherine Creedon

Silliness

In attempt to let their personality and humor soak through the cotton-bound paper, many applicants try to make their cover letters funny. But these attempts rarely work. You have no way of knowing if your prospective boss shares your sense of humor. More broadly speaking, the cover letter offers a sample of your ability to conduct business-like communications. Clowning around can disguise your professionalism.

Poor grammar and, mispelings

No one wants to make grammatical or spelling errors, but applicants nevertheless consistently submit cover letters with small, thoughtless, yet deadly errors.

Many problems slip through because people have a difficult time seeing the mistakes in their own writing. So ask someone else to proofread the cover letter for you. If that's not possible, read the document aloud, slowly and word by word. Every time you make a correction, read the whole document over again. Writers make many mistakes during the final editing process as they make corrections, particularly with tense and word placements. Spell checks can also be typo insinuaters, causing writers to change misspelled words into wrong words, as demonstrated by one cover letter writer who boasted that "Referees are available on request."

THE SENTENCES IN THIS SAMPLE LETTER PROBABLY MADE SENSE TO THE WRITER AS SHE WROTE THEM, BUT READ THEM OUT LOUD AND LISTEN FOR AWKWARD CONSTRUCTIONS, GRAMMATICAL ERRORS, AND RUN-ON SENTENCES

Ava Strepto
50-32 31st Avenue #1B
Woodside, NY 11377
(718) 204-2113
December 29, 2003

I am actively seeking an opportunity for enhanced career growth — ideally, a challenge in which my administrative abilities could be utilized to there fullest. Increasingly responsible experience has enabled me to develop the kinds of experience that I would bring to any position. One particular characteristic of my work has been the degree of initiative that has been required and that, in fact, I have demonstrated, and my colleagues have continued to recognize my professional skill and facility at meeting organization objectives.

I am a highly organized individual who is able to juggle many different types of tasks simultaneously, as evident in my current position.

For your review I have enclosed my resume that summarizes both educational qualifications and work experiences to date.

I fully realize that this brief letter can not describe either the range of benefits I would bring to any position or the types of results I would hope to produce. Therefore, I would greatly appreciate the opportunity of speaking with you personally at your earliest convenience.

Sincerely,

Ava Stepto

Clichés put egg on your face

It goes without saying that the best way to sound unremarkable and insincere is to fill your cover letter with clichés. So if that's what you were planning, go back to square one and get busy as a beaver at putting together a collection of original thoughts instead of a collection of those same old employee buzzwords. Even if those buzzwords represent honest information you are trying to relay, remember, the road to hell is paved with good intentions. The best way to express your desires is to say how you really feel. True statements run circles around cliched phrases. So if you come up with the real McCoy, take a bow, because you're moving in the right direction faster than a speeding bullet.

Pontificating with immoderately labored interpretive phraseologies (that is, writing overdone sentences)

Sometimes, in an effort to impress, writers go overboard. How many times have you seen someone strain to play it cool, only to crash and burn after misusing an impressive-sounding word? In an attempt to sound intelligent, cover letter writers regularly produce sentences that use big, impressive, but unfamiliar words. The resulting mistakes cause embarrassment for both the reader and writer, and ensure prompt dismissal of your application. (Even if the reader understands your meaning, she may be put off by your pretentiousness.)

Egomaniacal tone

A golden rule for cover letter writing: make sure that by the time you've finished your writing, the person most impressed by your letter isn't you. This is an opportunity for you to give employers an idea of who you are, what you've accomplished and how you can contribute to their company. Nobody likes a self-absorbed narcissist, and even fewer people want to work with one. The best way to avoid such errors is to avoid unqualified, grandiose statements and assumptions about how impressed your reader will be with you.

AN INCREDIBLY ARROGANT COVER LETTER

JANE MUNRO
GRP Corporation
509 Sunset Way
San Francisco, CA 33009

July 1, 2003

Dear Jane:

I am extremely interested in the position you posted on Jobtrack for a legal assistant. Your list of qualifications might as well be my biography, so I am extremely optimistic that you will at least grant me an interview. I graduated from UC Santa Cruz in 2001 with a B.A. in both political science and english. Attached is a copy of my transcript, showing that I earned a 3.58 overall G.P.A., and a 3.79 with high honors in my strongest field: political science. I will be applying to law school next fall, and attending in the year 2004 without question.

I already have a good job. I send out my resume only for spectacular positions such as yours. I make $40K a year with full benefits and a matching 401(k) plan at 30 hours a week right now. I love what I do and where I work, I would, however, put in my two weeks notice immediately for your position. This is the most lucrative time of year at my restaurant so it would be only an opportunity such as this that I would be willing to let it all go. The opportunity to work in a legal setting before I return to school is, however, very attractive to me. The salary you are offering is adequate as well. I sincerely hope to hear from you this week or early next. I realize that the position has been posted for some time now and am sure that some good candidates have come to your attention already. As my schedule is very flexible, I am willing, of course, to come down for an interview ASAP. Please feel free to contact me at any time if you are as interested as I am. Thank you for your attention.

Martin Kelly
630 Nine St.
Oakland, CA 94617
(510) 884-9552

It's the sentiment that counts

When you tell potential employers why you're interested in working for them and their companies, be sincere. Don't bother pouring on a bunch of flattering statements. If you're interested in a position or company, just say why.

Okay:

"Cymad's increasing stake in the booming semiconductor market makes this position intriguing indeed."

"I've admired your company's products for some time, especially the Nibok 5000."

No good:

"You have the most fabulous company ever and it would be the culmination of my life dream to work with you."

"I would DIE to work at Microdex."

Silly time

If you're going to be silly, at least be witty. Some very creative industries and companies might indeed look favorably upon a cover letter like the following. At the very least, it'll grab attention.

WOULD SOMETHING LIKE THIS WORK FOR YOU?

Marketing Director
Puzzles Puzzles Puzzes Inc.
352 NE Labyrinthine Way
Hoopla, NY 10385

Dear Rupert:

This letter is to be sung to the tune of Old McDonald Had a Farm.

I'm interested in the position of marketing assistant. And feel I'd do a good job.
Last summer I had an in-tern-ship at Charles Schwab.

With a dedicated here. And an eager eager there. Here a dedicated. There an eager.
Everywhere a dedicated eager.

I went to Hollins-where I rowed crew. And majored in economics. My thesis was
published, and for the school paper, I drew political comics.

With a smart smart here. And a creative creative there. Here a smart. There a
creative. Everywhere a smart creative.

I feel I'd be perfect for this job. I'm always on the go.
When it comes to understanding what you need. I'll be in the know.

With the work work here and a hustle hustle there. Here a work. There a hustle.
Everywhere a work hustle.

I would love to come in for an interview. To talk about the position.
And to see if a match between us might come to a fruition.

With a thanks thanks here. For your time time there. Here a thanks, there a time.
Everywhere a thanks time.

Sincerely,

Paula-Foster Doe

INTERVIEWS

Overview

Congratulations. Your resume and cover letter wowed the gatekeepers, and you've been asked to come in for an interview. You've been given an opportunity to demonstrate, face-to-face, why you're the most competent and polished candidate for the job.

If the prospect of the interview makes you nervous, understand that it's perfectly normal. Now use your nervousness. Harness that energy. Use it to your advantage. Remember that interviewing is a skill, not a talent you're born with. Techniques for putting together a successful interview can be learned and practiced, honed and perfected. If you feel you're not a successful interviewer now, you can always learn. And it's becoming increasingly important that you learn how to interview. In today's marketplace of shifting careers and temporary engagements, interviewing well is the key to moving on — and up.

Getting Ready

CHAPTER 9

Would a seasoned attorney stride into a courtroom on the day of an important case without having considered every angle of the case? Would a professional climber arrive in Kathmandu without provisions and maps of Mount Everest? Nope. If you want to sway the jury or reach the summit, you've got to go into the big event prepared. The same is true of going into an interview. Preparation is an essential part of the interview process and one that is easy to overlook or shortchange.

According to polls, most job candidates spend less than an hour preparing for their interviews. No one is going to make you prepare for an interview, least of all the people who will be asking the questions, so it's up to you to get ready on your own.

Unprepared interview subjects often give poor interviews, says Clift Jones, an account director at Bozell Worldwide Advertising. "One of the biggest mistakes people make is to come in with no agenda. They don't know why they want the job, anything about the unique strengths of the company, or why they'd be a good match. They're eager and little else. It's much more impressive if they've put a lot of thought into what they want from a situation and what they have to offer before they come in."

By preparing for the interview you'll be doing yourself a favor. Remember: more time spent in preparation means less anxiety on the day of the interview. It's a relief to have something relevant to say, a cogent question on your tongue, a collection of stories underscoring specific elements of your prodigious competence, when the interviewer's anticipatory eyes fall on you and it's your turn to speak.

In addition to alleviating pre-interview stress, being prepared has several other benefits:

- It shows the interviewer that you care enough about the position, the company, and the industry to research its current status and future.
- It suggests that once you're hired, your preparation for meetings and assignments will be equally as sound.
- It shows respect for the interviewer and the company he or she works for.
- It provides more opportunities for you and the interviewer to have a meaningful conversation in which you can find common ground.

Research

Research is a vital preparation tool. Over time, companies, like countries, develop distinct cultures and inner languages. In some cases the language of a corporation or industry can become so specialized that an outsider will have trouble understanding it. The job candidate who learns an organization's lingo well enough to speak it during the interview just might, like a long-lost relative, be embraced with a cry of, "He's one of us!" and welcomed into the fold.

Where can someone find this kind of insider knowledge? Vault produces a series of profiles and surveys on organizations that can help the information-hungry interviewee. Other user-friendly, if more company-friendly, sources of information include the packets prepared for a company's stockholders. Any stockbroker will send you these, provided you assure them of your interest in someday purchasing stocks through them. A company's human resources, treasury, or public relations office will be happy to send you an annual report (which will include a company's financial, marketing, and product report), a prospectus (which includes a list of the CEO and major players), or a 10K report (which contains a company's historical and financial information).

Trade magazines, (or "the trades") industry insider magazines, can apprise you of current events, hirings and firings, trends, and other relevant issues. Libraries, career centers, and web sites can also be valuable information-gathering places. Spending a day at the library is an especially good way to get the job search going if you're just starting out.

Perhaps the most direct way of getting the real skinny on a company is to talk to someone who works there. Speaking to someone in a position similar to the one in which you're interested, can give you vital insights into the company's modus operandi and expose some of the rats in its cellar — or executive suites. If you don't know anyone who's had experience at the company, you might ask around to see if you have any less obvious connections to the industry or a parallel field.

As in other areas of the job search, it's a good idea to treat your preparation for the interview as a job. You might, for example, want to keep a notebook for observations on the companies with which you've interviewed. Or, you might collect the information you gather in an interview folder. Not only will this give you some practice — a warm-up in the organizational skills important in any job — but it will also help you focus and take the preparation process a little more seriously. Some especially important things to remember are the names, numbers and extensions of any contacts with whom you've spoken, the dates and times when those contacts occurred, lists of reasons why you're interested in a particular organization, and potential obstacles or drawbacks associated with a company.

Review your resume

Before the interview, your resume is probably going to be the only thing the interviewer knows about you. In most cases, whoever is going to interview you will have that resume close at hand and might even have memorized key elements of it, so it's important you to be totally familiar with what you've written. Take some time to review what you've done and to observe how it's represented. If you haven't updated your resume in a while, you might discover serious omissions. Maybe you've left off an important experience, or maybe you've forgotten about an experience that could take center stage during the interview. If you can't remember something on your resume, your interviewer may think you are lying.

Check the dates of past jobs for any gaps you might be asked to explain. If you were out searching for the last living grizzly bear in Arizona for those few months when you weren't working, spend some time thinking about how you can turn this to your advantage in the interview. Those tracking skills might prove your passion, bravery and tenacity, for example. Just as importantly, this offbeat experience might help you establish a connection with your interviewer and give him or her an insight into your character.

Consider doing some role playing as you review your resume. Try stepping outside yourself and look at your resume hypercritically, as an employer looking to hire you would. Based on your resume, try imagining questions you'd ask yourself and reasons for not hiring yourself. Once you've imagined the on-paper preconceptions this person likely has of you before you meet him, you can come up with an effective plan for exceeding these expectations face to face.

Because computers play such a vital role in the workplace, it's a good idea to review before the interview exactly which programs you know. If you have experience with any of the programs the company uses, you can make an immediate positive impact on the organization. If you're particularly ambitious, you can give yourself this computer advantage by finding out which programs the company uses and familiarizing yourself with them before the interview.

Emotional preparation

Even if you've made yourself into a walking tome of facts and figures, computer programs and trade lingo, you might not make a good impression unless you're emotionally prepared for the interview. In a mad rush to do whatever you have to do to land a job, you may not take the time to ask yourself how you really feel about this job.

The interview is as much a forum for you to find out if the company and the job fit your needs as it is for the company to discover whether or not you're right for them. You may have to give up some aspects of your dream job, but the goal is to sacrifice as little as possible. What do you want from a job? What are you good at doing? What do people compliment you on?

In the ideal situation, the interviewer and the interviewee are equally interested in finding a perfect fit. Look out for yourself. Ask hard questions about work conditions, drawbacks, and low points. If asked tactfully and backed up with research, well-directed questions of this sort won't offend a responsible interviewer. After all, a happy employee is going to be more productive than someone who hates his job.

But if you choose unwisely the first time, don't worry — jobs are no longer forever. People change careers nowadays about as often as their hairstyles. Chances are, even the person who interviews you, if he or she hasn't been living in a cave with blind fish, will understand that you probably won't be with the company for life. Gone are the days of the 1950s "company man" who signed up after college and stayed on until he retired. Nevertheless, choosing a job and career right the first time saves a lot of time and angst.

The following are some questions you'll want to answer, either by yourself prior to the interview or during the interview, to avoid ending up in the wrong position:

What are the hours?

If your research hasn't revealed this already, you should ask if a job advertised as 40 hours a week really takes 50 or 60 hours a week, or more. You have a right to know how much you'll be working and should protect yourself by asking in the interview whether or not this is truly a 40-hour-a-week job. Interviewers should be honest with you about this; it's information you need to know in order to make a good decision. If you're going to be slammed with work from nine to nine every day, it might not be worth it for you.

Pay?

Be aware that overeagerness to ask about salary can make you look unprofessional. Asking about salary while calling up to schedule an interview is a bad idea. The best time to ask about salary is after you've gotten the job, but before you've accepted. Even if money is your prime motivation, wait till late in the interview to ask money questions.

Still, salary and other benefits are important. Before you go in for an interview, think about how much you need to make to live comfortably, and how much you think you deserve to make, given the responsibilities and your qualifications.

What type of work will I be doing?

Before you go in for an interview, think about which type of work environment suits you best. As we saw earlier, different corporations develop different attitudes. The atmosphere on the floor of the New York Stock exchange is very different from a public library in a small town. Some jobs require you to work with a team in order to produce a final product, while you'll work in solitude in others. It's your responsibility to find the environment that best suits you.

How long will I be here?

Before the interview, you'll also wish to think about your commitment to the job. The interviewer will be concerned about how long you will be able to stay with them. Are you looking for summer employment between school terms, for a six-month experience, a three-month internship, or a lifelong career path? In establishing a career, consider that anything under a year does not constitute a valid work experience to some employers. In many jobs it takes six months just to get up to speed.

Are there walls?

When you go in for the interview, be alert to the work environment, both physical and human. Pay attention to the way the company gets its work done. Imagine yourself coming into that building every day. Do people in the office wear Armani or Levis, DKNY or Dickies? Do they crowd into cubicles or kick back in plush, well-ferned offices? Is there a backslapping, good-ol'-boy, "see the game last night,

Joe?" feel to the place? Do the workers seem happy or do they wander round the office like zombies? Are there stains on the carpet, interesting art on the walls? If you look at the interview experience as an opportunity to gather as much information as you can about the company, you'll have plenty of factors to sift through when it's time to make a decision.

Will I still be able to buy fresh bagels?

Before the interview, you should solidify your feelings about where you want to live and how flexible you are about relocation. Many people would gladly take an average job in Aspen or Bermuda over a fantastic one in Mayberry. It's up to you to decide how much place matters to you. Do you require the stimulation of a big city, or are you happier sitting on a front porch listening to crickets on a Friday night? In the most competitive professions it might be necessary to sacrifice location to win any position at all. In the fierce contests for tenure track jobs in academia, for example, it might be necessary to take the job at Mayberry Tech to establish a career.

Big fish in small pond or cog in machine?

How big a company do you want to work for? Will you be more comfortable as a prominent player in an office where everyone knows one another, or as a single, relatively unnoticed cog in a massive corporate machine? Smaller companies are more likely to offer flexible hours and vacation policies, and they may offer more opportunities for immediate, diverse, and substantive involvement. In addition, a smaller company may be a growing company. It can be exciting to ride a company as it grows, to watch and participate in the formation of its culture and lingo. Smaller companies also tend to suffer less from bothersome bureaucracies, so your ideas have a better chance of immediate implementation.

By the same token, it's difficult to hide in a small company. Everyone will soon realize if you're not producing. It may be more difficult for you to take vacation, or even a long lunch. Small companies also tend to pay less and can't offer the benefits of a larger firm. And especially in these consolidation-crazy times, they're somewhat more susceptible to buy-outs and bankruptcy than a big, established operation. Fortune 500 companies, on the other hand, can usually afford higher salaries than smaller places can. They also offer more comprehensive benefits. and may offer a wider variety of potential places to live.

In the interview process, employees at small companies understand that they don't have the name recognition of bigger places and won't expect you to know as much about them. This is why it's an especially good idea when interviewing with a smaller place, to find out who they are and what they do. Make sure you thoroughly check their web site, if they have one. At least research the industry in which the company's involved if you can't find anything more specific.

To help you determine what is the perfect job, we've designed a test that can help you think about how you feel about a potential job. First, answer the "Jobs in General" section of the quiz, which asks you what you want from your perfect job. Then take the quiz again, in the "Specific Job" section, based on the specific job you're up for. After you've entered all the numbers, subtract the specific from the general job score. As in golf, the goal is to have as low a score as possible.

Controlling jitters and tension

The prospect of sitting alone in a room with a stranger and talking about yourself can be terrifying. You certainly don't want the stress to overwhelm you. If an interviewer's strongest impression of you at the end of the interview is the sweat on your brow, quiver in your voice, and the twitches in your limbs, you're in trouble. Here's how to put things in perspective.

Remember:

- Someone at the organization likes you and thinks you have a chance to contribute. You've haven't been called in to be tortured — you have a real shot at getting hired.
- If this interview doesn't work out, you will have another one. There are a lot of jobs out there.
- Every interviewing experience you have will prepare you to do better in the next one.
- The person sitting across from you was once sitting on the hot seat just like you, and they survived and got the job even though their voice trembled a bit and their knees knocked a little. Everyone's been through the situation and knows what it's like.
- Just like everyone else, this person interviewing you has friends and casual acquaintances with whom they hang out. They aren't always so formal. Try to connect with your interviewer on a human level, without being too goofy and informal.

The practice interview

Artists apprentice themselves to masters, professional sports teams play scrimmages and actors conduct dress rehearsals. Practice creates (hopefully good) habits, makes movements instinctual, converts decisions into instant reactions. With something potentially life-changing as an interview, leave as little as possible to chance by conducting one or more practice interviews. Certainly, you can't write a script for your interviewer (wouldn't it be great if you could?) but you can prep for an interview much in the same way that you would study for a test.

Think of the practice interview as a dress rehearsal, as close a facsimile to the real thing as possible. An interview is typically a few shades more formal than ordinary interaction. You should make your practice interview reflect this formality. If you're going to wear a suit for the real interview, you should wear a suit for the practice as well. If you're going to wear velvet knickers, an orange wig, a rhinestone blazer, and oversized pea green sunglasses, wear these for the practice. Arrange to meet your mock interviewer in a neutral space, preferably an office setting, at a specific time. Whoever is playing your interviewer should remain in character for the entire interview, no matter how tempting it might be to crack a joke or ask a goofy question. (Many universities offer mock interview sessions to students and alumni, and some professional clubs will do them as well.)

Immediately following the mock interview, discuss your performance. (At some mock interviews, the conversation is taped and replayed, which can be helpful). Begin with physical observations and work in to the substance of your answers. You might be amazed at what an objective observer will notice about you — things you never realized you were doing, such as raking your fingernails over your pant legs, playing with your earlobe or continually shaking the hair out of your face when it's not there to begin with. And remember, these quirks often grow more intense with nervousness. In general, remember to keep your hands below your shoulders during an interview. Scratching your neck, playing with your hair — all distracting little tics you should control.

The practice interview is also a good place to monitor and adjust the volume and speed of your speech. You don't want to have to repeat yourself or to have the interviewer cover his or her ears when the full force of your nerves gets behind your voice and you blurt out those answers at a volume that frightens even you.

Dealing with anxiety

It would be a shame to let something as insignificant and short-lived as an attack of nerves conceal your winning attributes. Here are some tips to prevent nervous tics and other imperfections from interfering with your best interview ever.

- If you're concerned with a piece of clothing in your interview ensemble — maybe the naked-lady tie is a little racy and you're on the fence about it — change it. In addition to favorably impressing your interviewer, your clothes should do nothing but support and feed the confidence and comfort of the intelligent, sensitive creature wearing them.

- During the interview you'll want to look neat, clean, and well-composed. You should always wear a suit. Even if the workplace where you're applying is business casual (or has no dress code whatsoever.) Even if the interviewer tells you that you don't need to wear a suit. It's always better to overdress than underdress. Stick to conservative navy, gray or black. Women, wear pantyhose and closed-toes shoes.

- If a deficiency on your resume worries you, don't obsess on it and let it sink your spirits. Think about this deficiency and how you will explain it before you go in for the interview. It's there, so deal with it and move on. Remember, they've agreed to interview despite this flaw, so it can't be a stopper. If there is any way of putting a positive spin on it without making it a feature of the interview, plan a short but sweet response.

- On the day of the interview, breathing exercises can help you relax and focus your energy. Close your eyes, imagine a peaceful place. Or, visualize yourself acing the interview. Here's another one:

place your tongue at the roof of your mouth just behind the teeth and then breath quickly and forcefully through your nose for as long as you can. If you push yourself at this, when you then inhale deeply through your mouth again, you should feel energized.

- Carry a pen into the interview with you and squeeze all of your stress into the pen. Do not chew on it.
- Bring a pad of paper to take notes.
- Carry a briefcase or leather portfolio.
- Women: buy extra hose, in case the pair you plan to wear rips the morning of the interview.

T-minus 24 hours

Make sure you get plenty of sleep the night before the interview. Before you go in, make sure you've had plenty to eat and drink — preferably brain food like fruit, vegetables and fiber — but at least eat something so that you'll be operating at peak thought and coordination. It's also a good idea to eat before you get into in your interview attire. You don't want to spray spaghetti sauce on your white shirt or drip grape juice on your only clean suit.

For your own peace of mind, get to your interview site early. Give yourself a 30- to 45-minute window. The last thing you want is to have to start off the interview with an apology for being late. If you can, go to the building the day before your interview and scope it out. See how long it takes you to get there and give yourself more than enough time the next day. Even if you can't make a trial run the day before, give yourself enough slack so that you can go to the door and walk away. Hang out in your car and listen to relaxing tunes. Go for a stroll around the neighborhood, or find a soothing place to wait. Then enter the office approximately 10 minutes early.

Once you're in the office, treat everyone you meet with respect and courtesy. Don't snub the receptionist. Introduce yourself and mention the name of the person you're there to see and the time of the appointment. Run to the bathroom and check yourself out. Make sure there is no toilet paper in your shoe. Then, take a seat. Do not start eating anything. Pretend to read company literature. Wait.

At the Interview

CHAPTER 10

The meeting and small talk

If you're old enough to be vying for a job that requires a serious interview, you've probably met a lot of people in your life. Extend those social skills to the people in the office. Maintain solid eye contact and a firm handshake. This proven greeting combination implies strength, confidence, competence, and honesty. Consider the alternative: shifty eyes and a limp handshake.

After the initial meeting and a stroll back to the interview room, the next phase of the interview begins — small talk. The interview hasn't officially begun, but make no mistake: your ability to talk about the weather is being measured up. The topic of conversation might in fact be the weather, a brief discussion of the latest media frenzy, the game last night, a round or two of the name and geography game. Small talk is meant to relax you, so allow yourself to be relaxed. Remember though, that you're still in an interview and anything you say can be used against you in the decision process. Answer small talk questions briefly, honestly, diplomatically and tactfully. Be witty, but not obscene or clownish.

The main event

At some point, the interviewer will shift to the heart of the matter and begin to ask questions pertaining to the job and your fitness for it. Often these questions will follow a description of the available job and an explanation of the company and what it does.

Often the segue from the small talk session into the more serious portion of the interview will be marked by a description of what the company does. Your interviewer might ask you what you know about the company, and after you give your answer (astute and detailed, due to your extensive research) the interviewer will talk about the company, the job, the industry, their plans for the future. This is a good time to demonstrate your listening skills. Let them see that you're listening and interested and pay attention to what they're saying. Take notes on the notepad you remembered to bring.

Focus

Before anything else is said it might be helpful, here, to dispense an all-purpose interviewing bromide: remember to focus. Once the middle, substance portion of the interview begins, the interviewer is primarily interested in your past job performances and possibly your life performances in as much as they relate to the open job. He or she wants to know how your experience and personality will translate into the available job. For example, when the interviewer says, "Tell me about yourself," they're interested in your work experiences, not the fact that you were born in deepest February when the moon was on the wane, and frost obscured the windowpane. Your interviewer will be thinking of little else except whether or not you will be able to do the job. (This does not mean that you should purge yourself of all personality — it's fine to mention that you like ice fishing — but you should keep your eye on conveying your fitness for the job.)

During the interview you should act like a boxer in the ring. You want to land as many substantive punches as possible. You want every one of your answers to count. If you use up a lot of your time and energy on false punches — statements that fail to focus on the job and why you're a good person to fill it — the interviewer is going to decide you're wasting time. If you feel yourself getting off topic and talking about something that's not really relevant, it's all right to mention this. Your interviewer will appreciate the fact that you reined yourself in — this demonstrates control, maturity, an understanding of the bottom line, and well-developed communication skills.

Honesty

Any lies you tell about your background and accomplishments will come back to haunt you. Similarly, unless you're an experienced actor, any affectations in attitude or manner will be detected by an experienced interviewer. Interview situations are stressful enough; you don't need to add method acting to the mix. Be honest without dwelling on your weaknesses. Be the best version of yourself. Practiced interviewers will appreciate your candor. They'll know they're dealing with an honest person.

Who's doing what for whom? It is better to give than to receive

Often, an applicant will blithely run through a litany of reasons why the position fits his career paths without mentioning what skills, insights, or vision he can bring to the position. It's a good idea to steer clear of this trap. Often when thinking of a position, especially one that is perfect for our career aspirations, we do tend to think about it in terms of what it has to offer us. Your love for the position, however, should not be the focus of the interview. The spotlight, from beginning to end, should shine on the myriad reasons why you'll be indispensable to the company once you're in the position.

Finding common ground and bonding

Employers, being human, will often hire someone they like — someone who reminds them of themselves at the same age, or someone to whom they are connected in whatever way — instead of the person who will perform best in the job. It's far more difficult to turn a friend down for a job than it is to nix someone about whom you have no particular feeling. So try subtly and deftly (it's easy to go overboard and become an Eddy Haskell) to form a connection with the employer.

If you can discover what kind of person you're dealing with, what his or her passion is, it will be easier for you to become a bit of a chameleon for bonding purposes. Any connection you can discover with the person can help. Find a topic such as a shared alma mater or an outside interest upon which you can build a connection. Do what you can to size the person up. If they mention a hobby or a recent vacation, express real interest. If you can get them to like you as a person, in addition to making them feel you're the best candidate for the job, you'll have done yourself a tremendous favor.

Making an end run

Trying to use humor or other methods of endearment in an interview is risky, but so are most business ventures. Similarly, being completely straightforward in the interview holds risks, but telling the emperor he has no clothes might impress some interviewers.

We all know at least one person who has a knack for making immediate connections, one of those people who never meets a stranger. But the ability to establish an instant rapport with someone can be learned. Think about those people in your life who have a knack for meeting people. What are their secrets? How do they do it? Are they able to project a genuine enthusiasm, a guilelessness that disarms people? While it can be dangerous to try to take on someone else's personality for an interview, try to discover ways you can better connect with someone. The following is a list of things you might want to keep in mind by way of forging a bond with your interviewer.

- Listening. Remember your grade-school teachers. "Don't just listen. Show me you're listening." Let the interviewer see your interest and enthusiasm. Concentrate on what they're saying.
- Read 'em and weep. Or make 'em laugh. Try to discover what motivates your interviewers. What kind of person do they look like? How are their offices decorated? Do some research on your interviewer. Find out who they are and what they do outside of work. What are their hobbies and passions? It's amazing how much even the most reserved person will open up if you find the right subject.
- If they're trying to be funny, don't be too nervous to laugh.

Asking for the job

If you know you want the job, don't be afraid to let the interviewer know this, point blank. If an interviewer senses wishy-washiness, they'll offer the job to someone else. They want to hire someone who wants the job, not someone who will grudgingly accept it. Express interest in the position and the company.

Questions to expect: The quality search

Interviewers, inevitably, seek the ideal candidate. To become this perfect hire, put yourself in the mind of the interviewer. Take a good look at yourself. What does this person look like? How does this person dress, and carry him or herself? Which qualities does this interviewee demonstrate in his or her answers?

Increasingly, interviewers will ask behavioral questions — questions that seek to understand you through the prism of your past behavior and accomplishments.

One cool customer

If you're the person who can step into the bloody heart of the fray with ice water in your veins when the office resembles Custer's camp on the Little Bighorn, then you'll be a valuable asset to the company. If, on the other hand, you get frazzled when someone asks for the company's address, you might be a dangerous liability when the bullets start to fly and scalps are being taken. So your interviewer is going to be watching you to see how you handle the stress of the interview and your ability to remain composed. The following are some questions you should know how to answer by the time you're sitting in the hot seat:

1. You're in customer relations and an unsatisfied customer is complaining bitterly about the product or service. How do you handle the situation?
2. You've been given multiple tasks. There is no way you can complete all of them on time. What do you do?
3. Describe some situations that really bother you.
4. You're right. You know you're right. And, yet, everyone is taking issue with what you say. How do you react?
5. How well do you handle pressure in the workplace?

How bad do you want it and what will you do to get it?

During the interview, one quality for which your interviewer will undoubtedly be searching — in your answers, handshake, appearance, and voice — is enthusiasm about the industry, the company and the particular job opening. They're counting on you to bring in a jolt of fresh-faced exuberance. You can express your energy and aggressiveness in the interview, but true excitement is difficult to fake. Here are some questions designed to measure the true level of your enthusiasm.

1. What do you feel are your best and worst qualities, and how will these relate to the position?

2. What interests you about this position, industry, organization?
3. What are your long-term career goals?
4. What motivates you?
5. How important is winning to you?
6. What is the most difficult thing you've ever had to do. Why?
7. Has anyone ever really pushed you? How did you respond?

Where you've been and what you've done

What you've done in the past serves as the clearest indication of what you'll be able to do in the future. If you can portray yourself in your interview as someone with a string of past successes by telling honest anecdotes in which you emerge as the hero, you're on your way to winning the job at hand.

Remember, however, that an experienced interviewer will be on to you like your first grade teacher if you try to snow him or her. Here are some questions you should know how to answer in the category of past performance:

1. Describe your duties at [this particular position].
2. Of which of your past accomplishments are you most proud?
3. What, based on your experience, have you found to be your optimal work conditions?
4. What are the most valuable lessons you've learned from past work experiences?
5. Which of the skills you've picked up at the positions listed on your resume do you feel will best translate into this position and why?
6. What are your long-term goals in this industry and at this company?
7. Describe a problem you encountered at one of your jobs and how you handled it.

Writing and rapping

These two arts form the bedrock of civilization and important skills for any job. Any experienced interviewer will be searching for soundness, if not outright eloquence, in written and oral communication. Your oral communication abilities will be on display, from the moment you meet the interviewer to the time you bid them adieu.

Your writing skills will be evaluated in the resume and cover letter, and sometimes, in a formal writing sample. Those mistakes on your resume — the misspelling of your own name, the missing dot in your e-mail address — will imply a dangerous lack of attention to detail and may be viewed by a potential employer as the tip of the iceberg. If this person can't manage these small details, he or she may think, then how will they be able to handle the larger requirements of this job?

It's a good idea to remember that communication extends beyond just words. Facial expressions, gestures, style and cleanliness of dress, tone of voice, posture, scent, and hairstyle send a message of one kind or another to your interviewer from the moment you stride confidently through the office door. So think about these questions.

1. Compare and contrast your oral and written communication skills.
2. What experience have you had with public speaking? In your view, what are the key attributes of a successful public speaker?
3. Let's say someone refuses or is hesitant to embrace your ideas. How do you persuade that person you're right?
4. What problems have you had with past employers and co-workers and how did you deal with these situations?
5. Describe the optimal work relationship between a manager and his or her employees.
6. What do you find most troubling about writing a research paper or giving a speech?

Sense of responsibility

Your interviewer is also going to be looking for a sense of accountability, a willingness to shoulder the burdens of the job. They will also be especially alert to any signs that you might not stay in the position long enough to make it worth hiring and training you.

A corollary to this sense of responsibility is whether or not you can be a self-starter. Employers are looking for self-sufficient workers — people who can produce for them from the word go. In the past, companies were interested in a worker for life. They welcomed people into the fold, trained them, nurtured them, and made lifelong projects out of them. In today's climate of short-term and shifting positions, employees at every level are expected to produce, to think creatively, and to make decisions about the organization's direction. Here's how your interviewer will try to determine if you have the right attitude.

1. Describe some ways in which you've been a leader.
2. What criteria do you use to make important personal decisions? Professional decisions?
3. Under what circumstances have people depended on you?
4. Describe the biggest setback you've dealt with. What was your response?
5. What, so far in your life, has given you the greatest satisfaction?

6. Do you prefer to have a lot of supervision or do you work well on your own?

How you think

The interviewer will want to measure how well you think on your feet, on your seat — how you think, period. How does that brain of yours channel and process information — rationally, creatively, sporadically? Companies prize the ability to think analytically. Many of the most successful people in business attribute their success to the fact that they surrounded themselves early on with intelligent people.

A number of questions in the interview will give you an opportunity to demonstrate how your mind gathers, sorts, files, and discards information. Sometimes the best thing to do when faced with a difficult question is to take a deep breath or to ask for a minute to consider it, instead of launching into a hurried, muddled answer. Especially if your answer is well considered, the interviewer will respect your decision to think it over more carefully.

In addition to being a necessary attribute on the job, possession of a rational thought process can be a tremendous asset in terms of getting a job. If you can offer an impeccably-reasoned, airtight case for why you should get the job, the interviewer, having difficulty refuting it, may simply surrender and hire you.

1. Describe the most creative things you've done in past jobs. In your personal life.
2. If you were hiring someone, what attributes would you define as being the most desirable and why?
3. What criteria did you use to determine your career path?
4. If we could form a perfect job for you within this organization, what would be some of the primary characteristics of this job?
5. What are the criteria you would use to determine success? How should a company determine success?
6. Describe your most rigorous intellectual challenge to date.

Ability to formulate effective plans

Efficient planning is paramount in most jobs. To demonstrate that you understand the importance of planning and organization, discuss past experiences, placing special emphasis on how you organized your approach to a specific problem.

The interviewer wants to test your ability to recognize and analyze a problem and to circumvent or solve that problem. Like the thought process questions, these questions are often more concerned with discovering whether or not you realize the value of organizing your plans than in the substance of the answer. Some potential planning questions:

1. What would you say is the difference between an organized and an unorganized office?
2. How do you plan to advance in this industry?
3. What are your long-term career goals? What are your long- and short-term plans for achieving them?
4. If you were in charge here, what would be your long-term plan for the organization?
5. What has the word "vision" meant to you?

Organization and attention to detail

In order to plan for the future, you've got to be organized enough to have the present situation under control. In an interview situation, organizational ability can be implied in the way you dress, groom yourself, and handle the papers you bring with you. (Even something tiny, like forgetting a notepad and having to ask your interviewer for note paper, can peg you, unfairly, as a slacker.) It can also be demonstrated in the way you carefully structure your answers by revealing your careful attention to process when describing past experiences.

Mastery of even the smallest details is a crucial part of any job. If a person can't master the smaller details, no matter what the position, they'll have trouble advancing in the industry. As mentioned, your resume and cover letter are good places to start demonstrating an attention to detail. There is no reason why these documents shouldn't be perfect. You don't want your career to be put on hold because you tripped over a misspelling in a cover letter.

1. How important are details to you? Why or why not?
2. What does it mean to you to be organized?
3. What role do you think organization plays or should play in this position?
4. How important has organization been to your past positions?
5. Are you naturally an organized person? If not, what steps do you take to organize yourself?

Flexibility

Stretch. Streeeetch. Many employers want to hire people who can wear many hats or who are amenable to working unusual hours under a wide range of pay arrangements. Usually, it's a good idea to convey a sense of flexibility in the interview. The employer might not be exactly sure how he or she wants to use you, so if you're too rigid in your job parameters, there's a chance you might just cull yourself right out of any job.

But there's a difference between flexibility and gullibility. Don't make any firm answers in the interview situation with regard to pay or hours. It's usually best to say you'll consider whatever they offer, unless it's completely out of the question. This approach will give you some time and distance to think more coolly about figures that come up. "Negotiable," is an especially good word to use with regard to pay and hours because it doesn't tell them that it doesn't matter at all to you nor does it nail down definite figures that might scare someone off.

It's equally important to demonstrate flexibility concerning the kind of work you'll be doing. Early on, embrace as many kinds of tasks and projects as your employers can give you. The more you know how to do, the more valuable you'll be in present and future positions. And especially during the interview, it's a good idea to let them know that you're open to a wide range of new experiences.

1. Do you have a problem with doing multiple tasks?
2. How much are you looking to earn?
3. Sometimes we help out the people in [Department X]. How would you feel about completing projects over there in addition to the ones here?
4. How do you feel about working extra hours on occasion?
5. What would be your optimal schedule?
6. How do you feel about wearing this clown suit?

People skills

By its very nature, the interview reveals how a person interacts with others. In some jobs, this ability plays a much larger role than in others. If the position requires working with beakers of rattlesnake venom in a phoneless warehouse deep in the Mojave Desert, people skills may not come into play. If, on the other hand, the position involves selling rattlesnake venom for pharmaceutical purposes or working in the customer services office of Rattlesnake Venom Inc., people skills will be of paramount importance. The ability to establish a long-term, trusting relationship with customers builds and maintains success. So your ability to deal with people in the best interests of the company, including people no one else wants to deal with, can be a coveted quality.

1. What do you like most about working with others? What least?
2. A customer calls in to complain about the product, demanding a discount. You suspect they aren't telling the truth. What do you do?
3. What does the word "service" mean to you?
4. What are you willing to do to make a client happy? Where do you draw the line?
5. Describe some of your strategies for dealing with difficult people.

Work ethic

The ability to belly up to a job and keep going all day long, week in and week out, is indispensable. Even with the emphasis on efficiency, automation, computers, and a hundred other shortcuts, there's still no substitute for a John Henry on the job, someone who's going to finish the job even if they sweat to death doing it. Here are some questions that key into how hard you work.

1. How does it make you feel if you don't get to finish a job?
2. What's the most difficult thing you've ever had to do in your life?
3. What does hard work mean to you?
4. Describe a time when you worked hard to achieve an on-the-job goal.
5. Place hard work in the hierarchy of qualities necessary to do a good job.

Win one for The Gipper

Are you a team player? Teamwork is a big buzzword among HR professionals. This quality, beloved by many high school coaches, is also a darling of most employers. Because many managers, especially in sales positions, like to see themselves as coaches and use motivational speeches similar to those you might hear in a football locker room, it's a good idea to be aware of the team player concept when you step into the office for your interview. Are you willing to sacrifice some of your own needs, desires, free time and glory, for the greater good of the team? Being a team player, especially in entry-level positions, means doing the dirty work while someone else gets the glory. But it also means not shouldering more of the burden than you can bear. It means evenly distributing the work and the resulting credit and wealth.

1. How well do you work with others?
2. Describe a situation in which you sacrificed your immediate needs for the larger good of a team.
3. Have you participated in any team activities? What were they and what did you learn from them?
4. How important is recognition to you?
5. What do the words "team player" mean to you?

Discretion

The interviewer will want to make certain of your trustworthiness with delicate information. All companies have trade secrets, but some are more secret than others. As long as you don't babble about internal secrets from your former employer during the interview you should be fine.

1. Can you keep a secret?

2. Have you ever been trusted with sensitive information? Describe the circumstances.

3. Describe a time you were loyal to someone even though it was difficult?

4. What would make you tell someone this company's secrets?

Illegal questions

Interviewers are legally barred from asking questions about your religion, color, race, national origin, marital status, sex, sexual orientation, childcare arrangements, or other family plans. Federal and State laws such as The Americans With Disabilities Act (ADA,) the Pregnancy Discrimination Act, and the Civil Rights Act of 1964 (Title VII,) which was amended in 1991, allow you to avoid discussing any of this information. The questions interviewers ask should focus exclusively on the position and your experience and qualifications for it. You do not have to reveal any private information that does not relate to your ability to perform on the job.

Your interviewer might not realize they're asking an illegal question. So if they do ask a question of this sort, you should make a decision about their intentions and whether or not you want to answer it. In some cases, the question might be innocuous enough that you'll feel comfortable answering it. If you don't wish to discuss something that you fear might wrongfully be used against you, then you should tactfully say that question does not relate to your abilities to perform the job, abilities that include x, y, and z.

Brainteasers

Many companies, such as high tech companies and investment banking firms, give applicants brainteasers to assess their analytical and creative talents. Anyone, after all, can come up with a canned answer to display their leadership and management skills — but fewer people can quickly come up with three solid reasons why a manhole cover is round. Whether you're applying for a technical, corporate finance or marketing position, expect to get a few of these beauties. Creativity, mental flexibility and speed are of paramount importance to high-tech firms, and one surefire way to test these qualities is through these slightly offbeat questions.

If you field one of these brainteasers, your interviewer may give you a time limit. Don't become flustered. Simply try to think through the question from every angle you can. Most questions require either logic, that ever-popular "out-of-the-box" thinking, or both.

1. A company has ten machines that produce gold coins. One of the machines is producing coins that are a gram light. How do you tell which machine is making the defective coins with only one weighing?

Think this through — clearly, every machine will have to produce a sample coin or coins, and you must weigh all these coins together. How can you somehow indicate which coins came from which machine? The best way to do it is to have every machine crank out its number in coins, so that machine 1 will make one coin, machine 2 will make two coins, and so on. Take all the coins, weigh them together, and consider their weight against the total theoretical weight. If you're four grams short, for example, you'll know that machine 4 is defective.

2. Design the ideal alarm clock.

Let yourself go! And try to relate your answer to the position you're applying for. If you're up for a technical or engineering slot, talk about how you would design or program the clock. If you're in a marketing interview, talk about how you'd market its features. And anyone in corporate finance should try to figure out what it might cost to produce this idealized clock. (Also, don't be afraid to be creative, or even a little bit silly — at the same time, don't imply that you have trouble getting to work in the morning!)

3. What is your hobby? What kind of product that does not exist today do you think would be most useful in your hobby?

Creativity and enthusiasm are highly prized at technology firms in all employees. Your ability to conceive of new products will be a bonus in an industry that is always producing new things.

The case question

Case questions are most commonly used in consulting interviews, but other industries use them as well. Companies in search of analytical ability and poise may ask these questions. Case questions will vary in their breadth or specificity — some may be more geared toward figuring out how an applicant formulates long-term strategy, while others will require candidates to perform specific tasks, such as pricing promotions for a product. They often take from half an hour to an hour to answer.

Sample case:

The brand launch: If we were looking to introduce a carpet cleaner to our line of products, how would you go about developing a business plan?

The brand launch is a common brand management case question. As with consulting case questions, interviewers are interested in what kinds of questions you ask, how you proceed from assumptions you make, and your understanding of market pressures. If the interviewee has experience in the industry, he or she can actually use numbers or information gained from previous experience, though this is of limited importance. Interviewers may be pleasantly surprised if you know the size of the carpet cleaner market, or the characteristics of the key competitors — but they certainly don't expect exact information. The important thing, as with consulting case questions, is to think aloud. "The first thing that you would do is to verbalize your thought process as much as possible," advises one veteran marketing manager. "Express how you're thinking of the market."

The logical place to start with this particular question would be the carpet cleaner market and its future. How large is the carpet cleaner market currently? Is it expected to grow in the next several years? What are the main potential competitors? What trajectories are those companies on — are they moving out of that market, or planning to expand? Have there been many new launches in the carpet cleaner market by other companies, and are more anticipated? Finally, where is carpet cleaner sold — in grocery stores, in hardware stores, in convenience stores — and how? Is it an impulse buy? Is it purchased in emergencies? Does it rest securely on shopping lists?

Candidates should then turn to the company's strengths and weaknesses in the carpet cleaner market. Does the company produce similar products, and therefore, possess a base of R&D expertise? Does the company have a distribution network in place? Is the company sitting on extra capital it can invest into a product launch? Does the company have a strong brand in a similar market (shower cleaner, for example) that can produce synergetic advantages in promotion? Make sure to identify the company's weaknesses as well. Perhaps the company mainly sells to teenagers, not normally a large market for carpet cleaner.

A diligent marketer will also consider broader issues. One major category of these are consumer preferences. Are homeowners now opting for hardwood floors and throw rugs rather than carpeting? How are professional carpet-cleaning services faring? Are there trends in carpeting that affect the cleaner business (perhaps easy-to-clean carpets are reducing the need for cleaners)? Another major concern for marketers are demographic trends. Are foreign markets beginning to consume more carpet cleaner? Is there a population that will soon be a user of carpet cleaners, or will soon stop using the product? While legal and regulatory issues may be less important to the carpet cleaner market than to, say, the pharmaceuticals industry, they are always a consideration. Are aerosol carpet cleaners no longer feasible because of environmental regulations? Are certain international markets subject to trade regulations that interfere with the sales of carpet cleaner?

When making assumptions, sound out hypotheses. For example, we know that the American population is aging, but we also know that as the American population ages, many oldsters are giving up their large homes and moving into apartments or even senior centers. Consider these factors, tell your interviewers what you believe these trends mean for the market, and include that as part of your overall strategic thinking. Stress that you know you may be wrong, and that if market research shows otherwise, your decisions and strategy would change accordingly. "You want to be able to take it and go with it," says one marketing manager who has worked for several major companies. "If you need to make assumptions, then that's OK."

Once you have gathered information about the situation to your satisfaction, determine your objectives. Because consumer trends are fickle, and technological innovation can quickly transform an industry, brand strategy should not stretch too far into the future. Suggesting a gigantic cost-intensive plan in the high-tech industry that may break even after eight years is the quickest way to disqualify yourself from a brand position. A five-year plan is a good, safe way to compromise the need for long-term strategy with the pitfalls predicting future strategy inevitably brings.

Interviewers may present you with objectives at the start of the case. If they don't, ask. If no objectives are proffered, funnel your thinking into three main areas: market share growth, financial performance, and brand identity. Your relative emphasis on each of these will of course depend on the information you garnered earlier. If the company has a great deal of capital, for example, and the carpet cleaner category promises strong growth, your goal will probably be to build market share at the possible expense of profits. If a demographic shift in consumers of your product is expected (for example, Gen-Xers are evolving into an important carpet cleaner market), you may concentrate on defining or redefining your brand image.

The guesstimate

Companies that require more technical, mathematical abilities may ask for a guesstimate, which requires you to produce an answer to a question like, "How many barbers are there in Chicago?" No one expects you to actually answer this question accurately; the interviewer is trying to see if you can think logically and mathematically.

Sample guesstimate:

How many gallons of white housepaint are sold in the U.S. each year?

THE "START BIG" APPROACH: If you're not sure where to begin, start with the basic assumption that there are 270 million people in the U.S. (or 25 million businesses, depending on the question). If there are 270 million people in the United States, perhaps half of them live in houses (or 135 million people). The average family size is about 3, so there would be 45 million houses in the United States. Let's add another 10 percent to that for second houses and houses used for other purposes besides residential. So there are about 50 million houses.

If houses are painted every 10 years on average (notice how we deftly make that number easy to work with), then there are 5 million houses painted every year. Assuming that one gallon of paint covers 100 square feet of wall, and that the average house has 2000 square feet of wall to cover, then each house needs 20 gallons of paint. So 100 million gallons of paint are sold per year (5 million houses x 20 gallons). (Note: If you want to be fancy, you can ask your interviewer whether you should include inner walls as well!) If 80 percent of all houses are white, then 80 million gallons of white housepaint are sold each year. (Don't forget that last step!)

THE "START SMALL" APPROACH: You could also start small, and take a town of 27,000 (about one ten thousandth of the population). If you use the same assumption that half the town lives in houses in groups of three, then there are 4,500 houses, plus another 10 percent, then there are really 5,000 houses to worry about. Painted every 10 years, 500 houses are being painted in any given year. If each house has 2,000 square feet of wall, and each gallon of paint covers 100 square feet, then each house needs 20 gallons — and so 10,000 gallons of housepaint are sold each year in your typical town. Perhaps 8,000 of those are white. Multiply by 10,000 — you have 80 million gallons. Your interviewer may then ask you how you would actually get that number, on the job, if necessary. Use your creativity — contacting major paint producers would be smart, putting in a call to HUD's statistics arm could help, or even conducting a small sample of the second calculation in a few representative towns is possible.

Your turn: What do you want to know?

After the substantial portion of the interview ends, the interviewer will typically give you a chance to ask questions. Don't relax. Failure to ask any substantive questions will make you seem uninterested and will raise questions about how much you've absorbed when the interviewer was talking about the company and the available position. It's a good idea to prepare three or four questions before you go in for the interview. This way you'll have something to say, in case awkward silence threatens. And these questions, since you've prepared them beforehand, will reflect any serious concerns you have.

But make sure your pre-planned questions don't cover something that's been covered. As an interviewer speaks, try to think of questions based on his or her statements. Then, when the time comes for you to ask a question, repeat what the interviewer said as an introduction to your question. This proves you were listening. For example: "You said that sales slump during August and September. Have you been able to discover why?"

Queries prompted by genuine interest trump anything dutiful. A few smart questions will leave interviewers with a strong impression of your intelligence and your continued interest in the job.

A grab bag of questions to ask:

1. How easily do people advance from this position? Where do they go from here?
2. What kind of performance would merit a raise or promotion?
3. Is this a good position to learn about this industry?
4. What do you see as some of the biggest drawbacks of this position?
5. How often do 40-hour weeks turn into 50- or 60-hour weeks?
6. Where will I sit?
7. What would you say is the most rewarding feature about this job?
8. Who would be my immediate supervisors?
9. Who would be the other members of my team?

10. What do you see as the future of this company?

11. What are the immediate market goals of this company?

12. What have been your favorite things about working here? Are there any drawbacks?

13. Do you offer benefits or stock options?

14. Why was this position made available (or created) and under what circumstances might it be terminated?

15. If you were to make a pie chart depicting the work in this position, what would it look like?

The Aftermath

CHAPTER 11

When the interview ends, leave the building as gracefully as you entered, making sure you're as cordial to people on the way out as you were coming in. As you decompress, take some time to review the interview while it's still fresh in your mind.

Ask yourself: how could you have better answered the questions? Where did you succeed? Where did you fail? What will you do differently next time?

In assessing the interview, don't let the fact that you didn't feel a connection with the interviewer frighten you away from a great job. And lastly, consider what you've learned about the company and whether or not, all things considered, it will be a good place for you to be.

A thank you note is essential. Get it in the mail the day after the interview. If competition between you and another candidate is intense, the thank you note just might be the extra bit of effort that propels you to victory. Avoid hyperbole and excessive enthusiasm. Keep your note cordial and brief. Thank the interviewer for inviting you to the interview. Tell the interviewer it was a pleasure to talk to him or her. Then mention something you learned during the interview and assure them of your continued interest in the position — that is, if you are still interested.

AN EXAMPLE OF A WELL-COMPOSED THANK YOU NOTE

February 14, 2004

Dear Ms. Abzugg:

Thank you for the opportunity to meet with you yesterday. I enjoyed talking to you and Mr. Troutman about the future of Heartland Candies and my possible future there. The visit has increased my interest in the marketing position we discussed and assured me of my ability to provide you with an immediate contribution.
Thanks again for your time. I look forward to hearing from you soon.

Sincerely,

Will Get

Follow-up calls can also provide that extra thrust over the job wall in some cases. But it's a good idea to assess the situation before you call. Calling can make you look over-eager and can, if overdone, turn off prospective employers. After interviewing with a large and busy company along with several other candidates, it's probably better to just send a note and wait for the response. And until prospective employers make their decisions, everything you say to them can be used against you at decision time.

For this reason, both calls and letters should be viewed as extensions of the interview. The last thing you want is for a clumsy follow-up call to dash a favorable impression of you. But a well-placed follow-up call or letter can give you an opportunity to state an idea you failed to mention in the interview, to position your name in their memories, to demonstrate perseverance, and to separate yourself from the majority of candidates who don't follow up. E-mailed thank you notes, if well-written, are entirely acceptable in all but the most conservative professions.

Recent trends

A big part of your preparation for the interview involves keeping your eyes and ears open to the latest trends and buzzwords in corporate culture. Reading the paper every day, talking to employees, and surfing the Internet can help you keep abreast of what's going on. Knowing what's going on can help you converse intelligently with employers. The following are some characteristics of the late modern workplace scene that are gaining prominence and will likely play an increasingly important role in coming years.

Behavior-based interviews

Since a Memphis psychologist coined the term 20 years ago, this form of interviewing has become enormously popular. The term refers to any interview that focuses on a person's specific past performances and experiences rather than one that asks general, hypothetical questions. This type of interview seeks to avoid generic, "canned" answers by asking for anecdotes from past work experiences that illustrate your competence. Behavior-based interviews also ferret out lies quickly. It's almost impossible to produce convincing details about a nonexistent experience.

Some career centers urge the "STAR" system in answering behavior-based questions. STAR stands for Situation/Task, Action, and Result and serves as an organizing framework for work-experience narratives. When answering behavior based questions, remember that interviewers are looking for someone who's optimistic, creative, a leader, and a team player. Never admit to not getting along with anyone, or facing a problem that vexed and defeated you. Do think of examples of times you made a concrete, positive contribution.

Multiculturalism in the workplace

It's no longer a white male world. Increasingly, women and people of color are earning positions of power, bringing to the table their unique perspectives and drawing from their experiences. Working harmoniously with people from a variety of cultural backgrounds has become a necessity in most corporate settings. If you're unable to accept people from a variety of backgrounds, you're going to have trouble thriving professionally.

International competition

Many companies no longer limit their thinking to one nation or world region. Along with traditional international outposts in Western Europe and Japan, booming markets are emerging in South America, throughout the rest of Asia and Russia. In the higher levels of company management, conference calls or video conferencing between people in several different countries have become common occurrences.

This new global perspective means three things for the interview.

1. You should highlight your ability to speak a foreign language, even if it doesn't seem immediately relevant to the job.
2. If the company has international interests, tell them if you're willing to work abroad, give reasons why you're interested, and explain why you'd be a strong international worker. Talk about any overseas exposure you've had.
3. You need an understanding of the global marketplace and what internationalization means for your company.

Post-hierarchy companies

Many of the corporations that once organized their managers in a pyramid hierarchy now set their managers in a pattern resembling athletes on a playing field. Since employees are more likely to leave the company sometime during their careers, they're now expected to perform a wider variety of tasks. As an interviewee, you should demonstrate an implicit understanding of this new structure. Let the interviewer know you're more concerned with your job duties than in moving up the ladder. And indicate your willingness to sacrifice some of your individual aspirations and glory for the good of the team.

Informational interviews

Before you invest the time and energy to go after a specific job interview, it's useful to gather information in a less-formal, low-stakes setting. Informational interviews are more preparatory tools than anything else — forums by which you can discover the nature of industry without the performance pressure.

Sometimes the most glamorous-seeming jobs can be the most mundane and vice versa. Informal interviews are also a good time to find out what a person's favorite and least-favorite aspects of work are. There's no way to find this out unless you seek out the people who do these jobs. Let's say, for example, you love books and decide for this reason that publishing is the industry for you. In an informational interview with an honest publishing maven, you might discover that enjoying books and going through some of the drudgery involved in putting them together are two different things. It's far better to discover this sort of information early in the process than to get a job and learn it over a few years.

Informational interviews are best kept to a half hour or less. As in a job interview, come prepared with cogent questions. The more you find out before the interview, the more productive your questions will be.

Some interviewing don'ts

We've talked a lot in this chapter about what to do, what to say, and how to act. But the truth is, if you've gotten an interview, you already have some quality or experience that interested your prospective employers. The job, to some degree, is now yours to lose. Here are some final tips to help you avoid that fumble.

In an interview, don't:

1. Blame poor performance on past employers, workplaces, bosses, or co-workers. Even if you worked for Satan in Hell, make an attempt to say something pleasant or neutral, such as, "I met many interesting sinners," or "It was a really hot industry."
2. Discuss personal or academic pursuits, unless you're still clearly in the small talk portion of the interview, someone asks you about these directly, or it you can relate them to the position for which you are interviewing. Hobbies like mountain climbing show persistence.
3. Appear too eager to discuss matters of compensation, hours, or vacation time. These are legitimate questions, but they should take a back seat to discovering whether or not you and the job are a good fit.
4. Show bad posture: don't slouch, tap your feet or splay your legs or arms.
5. Let nervousness alter your actions: don't fumble with objects in your hand, rearrange your hair, jiggle pocket change or chew gum.
6. Let your message get muffled: don't slur, don't drop your eyes, or speak too quickly.
7. Fail to have questions when the time comes.
8. Run on too long with answers to questions. Be aware of how the interviewer is responding to what you're saying. If you catch him or her looking bored or staring at you with a glazed or unfocused look, it's probably time to stop talking. If they want to find out more about what you were talking about, they'll ask you to continue.
9. Fail to answer the question you're asked.
10. Forget to smile! Remember, you're there at their invitation.

I accept

If the job you accept involves a number of agreements such as salary, health benefits, a 401(k), stock options, annual raises, vacation days, work hours, and travel, then your acceptance letter can confirm that you and your employer have a mutual understanding about your terms of employment. Subjects discussed in interviews and settled through verbal agreements can often be forgotten or misinterpreted, so you should clarify things now. Keep a copy of your acceptance letter.

The format for these letters is less rigid (since you already have the job, unless you send in some chicken scratch written on construction paper with crayon, you'll probably be fine), but you obviously want to start you new job on the best note possible. Here's a basic format that makes writing acceptance letters easy and effective:

First paragraph. Time for pleasantries. First, formally (and with great pleasure) accept the job you've been offered, making sure to list the exact title of the job you've been given. Tell them how much you enjoyed coming in and meeting them at the interview and how you're looking forward to working with them and the company.

Middle paragraph(s). Here's where you outline exactly what job you understand you're accepting. The type of work you'll be doing and the compensation you'll be given should be restated here to ensure an understanding between you and your employer. Try to avoid scary lawyer-ese prose; you don't want to spook your new boss with this letter. It shouldn't read like a legal contract, after all, but an assurance of mutual understanding.

Last paragraph. Time to give thanks to the people who made your employment possible. No, not your mom, and not "the little people." The people you want to thank are the people who gave you the offer: your employers. Then, tell them what day and time you will see them next: a polite way to confirm your starting date.

THE WRITER OF THIS LETTER SUCCEEDS IN TURNING A RUNDOWN OF HIS EXPECTATIONS INTO A GRACIOUS LETTER OF THANKS

July 2, 2004

Happy M. Ployer
Head of Development
Spread Over Land Development
777 W. Sunset Rd.
Kansas City, MO. 65984

Dear Happy:

It is with great pleasure that I accept your offer to fill the position of Acquisition Assistant. I enjoyed my interview very much and thank you for its positive outcome.

I am proud to be joining Spread Over Development starting July 16 with a salary of $28,000 a year. I am particularly grateful for the fully covered medical benefits, including a $10 deductible for medication. I am also pleased with the 10 days of paid vacation time.

I assure you that I will do my best to make my impact substantive and immediate. As I mentioned in the interview, I am especially looking forward to working with Sandy Schulman in the Development Office.

Sincerely,

Sam Spoon

No thanks

When the employer left your interview more impressed than you were, you'll be in a position to decline the offer they presented you with. You should first decline politely over the phone so the employer can offer the job to the next-best applicant as soon as possible. However, a true professional never lets any future networking opportunity turn into a dead end. Particularly in today's job market, in which employees flit between companies like pollinating bees, you need to keep your options open for the future.

In the following pages, we give examples of three different types of decline letters. The first writer has received a better offer, but her letter honestly and politely keeps the door open while inviting the first employer to sweeten the offer. The second letter is an outright turndown, but the writer's graciousness ensures that his interview can serve him well in the future. The third writer has withdrawn her name from consideration, but has briefly given her reasons for doing so, preventing herself from seeming flaky.

DECLINE LETTER #1

January 3, 2004

Heather Gull
444 Granger Pl. #9
Washington, D.C. 18888
321-444-8970
hgull@getum.net

Warren Nations
Manager, Missile Sector
Big Guns Munitions Factory
1010 Peaceful Shady Lane #3
Hanes, NM. 23451

Dear Warren:

As you know from our meetings and phone conversations, I am very excited by the prospect of working for Big Guns. Your sales and marketing team ranks among the best I have met in my job search. I found your plant is clean and efficient - and the natural beauty of New Mexico very alluring.

I am eager to accept your offer and begin working for Big Guns. However, I should tell you that I have received another offer of employment with Bombs, Bombs, Bombs in Cleveland, Ohio. While everything at your organization holds a greater appeal for me and my career, I must tell you that they have offered a salary $4,000 a year higher than your offer. Because I am concerned about paying student loans, this extra money is very welcome.

Instead of accepting their offer immediately, I wanted to reiterate my continued interest in Big Guns and to express my hope that we can come to terms on this matter and begin our happy association as soon as possible.

I eagerly await your response.

Sincerely,

Heather Gull

DECLINE LETTER #2

June 4, 2004

Gil Tuttle
Inside Sales
Computerama Tech
323 Industry Lane Suite 3
Seattle, Washington 98105

Doug Soren
333 Jones Ave.
NE. 42nd St. Apt. 2
Seattle, WA. 98105

Dear Gil:

Thank you for offering me a position on your sales team. While I have been impressed by what I have seen at Computerama Tech and enjoyed my meetings with you, I will not be able to join your staff, as I have accepted an offer at Databased Industries.

I appreciate your time and consideration, and after our interaction I feel very confident in using and recommending Computerama Tech products and services in the future.

Yours,

Doug Soren

DECLINE LETTER #3

May 7, 2004

Jesse Smith
Thoroughbred Magazine
222 S. Bluegrass Rd.
Lexington, KY. 40212

Shelly Equine
323 Twin Spires Rd.
Louisville, KY. 40209

Dear Jesse,

I am writing to ask you to withdraw my name from consideration for the position of writer. I have decided to pursue my freelance writing career full-time.

I enjoyed meeting everyone in the office. Thank you for your time and consideration. Best of luck in the coming year.

Yours truly,

Shelly Equine

Conclusion

You owe it to yourself to prepare as best as you can before stepping into the office. But remember, the interviewer will be basing his or her decision on surface observations. Hiring decisions remain subjective despite pretenses to the contrary. If you aren't selected, don't take it personally: you could have been up against the boss's nephew. Most importantly, don't carry any baggage with you to your next interview. Think of these interviews as a learning experience. Make a list of ways you can improve when the next opportunity comes along. Then move on.

If you do get offered the job, congratulations. Your preparation, research and practice paid off. If you decide to take the job, start on your letter of acceptance. If you're going to pass on the opening, make sure your rejection letter doesn't ruin the potential for a future relationship with the company.

But don't forget what you've learned here. The average professional changes careers six times in his or her lifetime. You've got other interviews in your future. But maybe the next time you interview, you'll be the one interviewing the candidates!

APPENDIX: RESUME MAKEOVERS

Introduction

It may seem unfair, but a few sloppy mistakes on a resume can ensure that it meets the garbage can swiftly. You don't want this to happen to you, do you? We've already discussed some of the ways you can immediately ensure that a resume looks good. Checking your spelling, discarding unnecessary information and discussing your previous experience in clear, focused, bulleted prose are all quick ways to make your resume look and read better.

But it's always easier to look at good resumes than improve your own, right? Wrong. With a little work, your lackluster resume can be transformed into a job-getting powerhouse. We took these actual resumes and turned them from meandering, misspelled, flabby documents into real resume knock-outs. Take a look and start beautifying your resume as well.

Remember that a great first impression is key. On average, a hiring manager weeds through 120 resumes for a single job opening. If you would like an expert resume to ensure that your resume stands out from the pack, have Vault experts review its content, focus, and presentation. Go to www.vault.com/careerservices/careerservices.jsp and get an expert resume review e-mailed to you within two business days. Or, have a Vault expert write the resume from scratch after a 1- to 2-hour interview with you.

ARDEN'S SLOPPY LAYOUT AND SCATTERSHOT TONE SINKS WHAT COULD BE A FABULOUS RESUME.

Arden Ward
13 Hemings Road, Jefferson, VA 22308
(703) 555-5529
ardward@aol.com

Production Assistant, December, 2002-Present. DD&E Group.

Daily responsibilities include proofing of pre-press material; art direction at photo shoots; photograph products for catalogs; working with service bureaus, printers and lettershops to provide start to production services; consulting; research for special projects; invoice tracking; shipping & receiving; distribution of completed job orders; writing job jackets; obtaining job quotes and sending client acknowledgements; inventory control; and database coordination for merge/purge files.

Lead Patient Registrar Coordinator. February, 2000-December 2002. Immobile Health Systems.

Supervisory responsibility for registration staffs and hands on job performance included but not limited to: Training and supervision of new and existing employees; created queries and production/maintenance of an electronic log. Responsible for production and distribution of weekly statistical data; data collection related to staff issues; compilation and written distribution of the same to management staff, liaisons, clinical coordinators, as well as, serve as a resource to numerous departments and maintain integrity of databases. Also, serve as back up to Administrative Clerk to handle general office duties.

Free Lance Graphic Artist, 1998-Present
Design and develop logos, letterhead, business cards, brochures, and flyers, as well as, offer consulting for the following companies: Balboza Consulting Services, Begone Press, Peritto Business Systems, and Data Farm, Inc.

Customer Assistant. June, 1997-July, 1999, Ameribanc Savings Bank.

Provided customer assistance on new and existing accounts. This included inquires, stop payments, blocks, holds, opening and closing accounts. Responsibilities also included answering phones, sorting and distributing mail to appropriate staff, faxing documents, review security tapes, daily balancing of the ATM machine, and the maintenance of customer account records. Organize branch promotions to solicit new accounts.

Assistant Manager, August, 1995-June, 1997, Fritz Camera Centers.

Involvement in overall operations including sales and film processing services. Specific responsibilities included customer assistance and sales, maintenance of equipment, inventory control, scheduling of personnel work load, and daily balancing of sales and receipts.

Education

A diploma from the School for Printing Specialist
Currently attending Billings Community College for a degree in Graphic Arts.

Summary of Hardware and Software Knowledge

Hardware
Database
IBM PCs
Peripherals
Access
Telecommunications
Windows

Software
Corel
Quark Express
Photoshop
WordPerfect
Windows NT
Carbon Copy
MS-DOS

LOOK AT HOW CLEAN ARDEN'S RESUME IS NOW!

Arden Ward
13 Hemings Road, Jefferson, VA 22308
(703) 555-5529
ardward@aol.com

WORK HISTORY

Production Assistant, December 2002-Present
DD&E Group.

- Art direction at photo shoots photograph products for catalogs
- Working with service bureaus printers and lettershops
- Consulting and research for special projects
- Invoice tracking; shipping & obtaining job quotes
- Proofing of pre-press material

Lead Patient Registrar Coordinator, 2000-2002
Immobile Health Systems

- Trained and supervised new and existing employees
- Created queries and production/maintenance of an electronic log
- Responsible for production, collection and distribution of weekly statistical data for management, staff, liaisons, and clinical coordinators
- Served as back up to Administrative Clerk to handle general office duties of various parties, including maintaining integrity of databases

Freelance Graphic Artist, 1998-Present

- Design and develop logos, letterhead, business cards, brochures, and flyers
- Consult on graphical issues for a dozen major companies

Consultant, Rotterdam Business Systems, 1999

- "Computerized" selective business organizations with hardware, software,
- Studied LAN and telecommunications
- Provided technical support
- Trained employees in use of PC applications
- Diagnosed hardware problems and cabling for Novell systems.

SUMMARY OF SKILLS

- Access
- Excel
- Lotus Notes 6
- Lotus Pro
- Macintosh Photoshop
- Microsoft Office
- MS-DOS
- Peripherals
- Quark Express
- Quattro Pro
- Sequel Solutions
- Windows Novell Netware

EDUCATION

A.B. in Graphic Arts
Billings Community College, Billings, VA
May 2001

CANDACE HAS ONE JOB BUT VARIED EXPERIENCE. SHE'S A PERFECT CANDIDATE FOR THE FUNCTIONAL RESUME

Candace Schmidt
250 Fourth Avenue
New York, NY 10101
(205) 555-9876
candys@yahoo.com

OBJECTIVE
Seeking a challenging position where previous skills, experience, and abilities will have valuable application.

QUALIFICATIONS
During my enlistment in the U.S. Army, I obtained training to include personnel management, physical security, weapons handling, secure information handling, and strategic planning. I am confident that my experience, interpersonal skills, and motivation qualify me as an ideal candidate for a number of positions.

WORK HISTORY

1996-2003 Infantry, U.S. Army
Supervised the training and activities of a five unit technical team. Directed complex operations. Evaluated the performance of those I supervised, then provided necessary counseling and remedial training. Instructed junior members of work team on various job related topics. Provided technical guidance to junior maintenance personnel. First-line supervisor, coordinating with senior personnel in the planning and execution of various administrative tasks.

Live weapons handling during routine training exercises. Qualified expert with numerous weapons. Trained in Urban Warfare, Physical security of valuable equipment. Personal quard. For a significant military official in a high security area. Operated communication and surveillance equipment in both emergency and non-emergency situations. Performed and supervised maintenance of heavy mechanical equipment and complex electronic devices.

Secured confidential information. Compiled various reports. Responsible for duty related files. Additional duties comprised of typing, filing, and accurate maintenance of records. Accomplished duties efficiently and accurately,

EDUCATION
U.S. Army Specialized training courses
Non-Commissioned Officers Course, 4 wks., 1999
Instructor Training Course, 2 wks., 1999
University of Toledo, Toledo, Ohio. 1995-1996

SKILLS
Sign -language, Interpreting//Communicating

REFERENCES
Available upon request

LOOK AT HOW GOOD HER RESUME LOOKS NOW!

Candace Schmidt
250 Fourth Avenue
New York, NY 10101
(205) 555-9876
candys@yahoo.com

Objective

I am seeking a managerial position in the retail industry that will make full use of my extensive supervisory and organizational abilities, and offer the chance for future growth and responsibility.

Education

U.S. Army Non-Commissioned Officers Course, 1999
U.S. Army Instructor Training Course, 1999
University of Toledo, 1995-1996

Experience

As a United States Army infantry member from 1996-2003, I employed the following skills:

Managerial and Instructional Skills

- Supervised the training and activities of a five-unit technical team.
- Instructed junior members of work team on various job-related topics.
- Provided technical guidance to junior maintenance personnel.
- As a first-line supervisor, coordinated with senior personnel in the planning and the execution of various administrative tasks.

Technical Expertise

- Supervised personal security for a significant military official in a high security area.
- Operated communication and surveillance equipment in both emergency and non-emergency situations.
- Performed and supervised maintenance of heavy mechanical equipment and complex electronic devices.

Administrative Experience

- Ensured the security of confidential information.
- Researched and compiled progress reports.
- Created, organized, and maintained division records.

Skills and Interests

Studying, interpreting and conversing in American Sign Language (ASL)

THERE IS NO EXPLANATION OF WHAT JOSEPHA HAS BEEN DOING SINCE 2001. THEREFORE, JOSEPHA SHOULD DEEMPHASIZE DATES IN HER RESUME. THIS RESUME IS SLOPPY AND CONTAINS NUMEROUS RESUME MISTAKES. THIS RESUME WOULD HIT THE GARBAGE CAN QUICKLY.

Josepha Whittier
9999 21st Street
San Francisco, California 94101

Objective: I am presently seeking a challenging career that my utilize my skills in Accounting, Payroll and General Offices ares

EXPERIENCE

2001-1997 Ennui Corporation, San Francisco, California
Accountant
Duties: Maintain domestic and international accounts for employees, vendors, insurance department and legal department.

1997-1995 Reptiliana, San Francisco, California
Controller/Office Manager/Bookkeeper/Secretarial/Receptionist
Duties: Perform accounting, payroll and general office duties.

1995-1990 Crunchy Company, San Francisco, California
Account Receivable/Receptionist
Duties: Perform account receivable and general office duties. Assist.

EDUCATION AND TRAINING

International Correspondence School, Scranton, Pennsylvania Accounting/Business

Bethany Corporation, San Francisco, California
Bethany Accounting Training Course/Business Management Course/Business Organization Skill/Computer Training Courses

San Francisco City College, San Francisco, California
Accounting/Data Programming/Criminology

San Francisco State University, San Francisco, California Domestic Law

Downtown High School, San Francisco, California Business

SKILL

10-key calculator, bookkeeping, answering phone, typing, copy machine.

COMPUTOR SKILL

Hardware: Apple / Atria/Compac/Digtal/Gateway 2000/Hewwellt-Packard/ IBM/IBM/Macintosh/Sony P.C./Tandy
Software: All-in-one/Dbase/E-mail/Internet/Lotus 123/Oak Street

THIS IS A SIGNIFICANT IMPROVEMENT FROM JOSEPHA'S PREVIOUS RESUME

Josepha Whittier
9999 21st Street
San Francisco, California 94101
(415) 555-4343
josephaw@aol.com

Objective: An accounting position that offers room for growth and makes full use of my extensive office, accounting and bookkeeping experience and education.

Education

College of San Francisco. 9/2001-8/2003
Graduate coursework in Accounting/Data Programming

San Francisco University. B.S. May 1990. GPA: 3.2
Major: Domestic Law

Experience

Accounting Experience
Ennui Corporation, San Francisco, California,1997-2001
As an accountant for Ennui, I maintained domestic and international accounts for employees, vendors and insurance and legal personnel.

Bookkeeping/Payroll Experience
Reptiliana, San Francisco, California, 1995-1997
I successfully handled multiple duties at Reptiliana, an extremely busy snake supply warehouse. My responsibilities included customer service, bookkeeping, payroll oversight and management of the entire office.

Crunchy Company, San Francisco California, 1990-1995
At the Crunchy Company, I both greeted and assisted visitors and customers, and assured that accounting and payroll records were timely and accurate.

Skills

Advanced bookkeeping, Lotus 123, Windows, Quicken, Excel. Well-versed in all computer platforms.

LOOK AT HOW UNFOCUSED JORDAN'S RESUME IS. HE INCLUDES A TRANSFER INSTITUTION AND OTHER INFO (LIKE HIS CHANGE IN MAJOR) THAT SINKS HIS RESUME. HE DIDN'T EVEN CHECK HIS SPELLING.

JORDAN HOPPER
2114 Muse Road, Ixnay, NY 07701, (732) 555-1352
Joho33@aol.com

Objective: A position in media and entertainment.

Education
FASHION TEXTILES UNIVERSITY
B.S. Degree, Merchandising Management, December, 2003
Lose comma between month and year
Marketing Club, Radio Club
3.5 GPA Presidential Scholar

CONVENT COMMUNITY COLLEGE
A.S. Degree, Marketing, 2002
One semester of Audio Recording before changing majors to Marketing.
3.7 GPA

Employment
GORILLA MUSIC
Assistant Manager/Part Time Manager, November 2002-current

Preparing the store for opening/closing, Training new employees,
Preparing Orders, Assisting Customers, Visual Marketing, Supervising
Employees, Inventory, etc.

FASHION FABRICS
Assistant Manager, October 2000-October 2002
Cashier, Floor Sales, Preparing Displays, Assisting Management with closing operations,
Including preparing bank deposits and the follow the following day's opening funds.

Ditto for Fashion Fabrics

ZUCKER HAIR DESIGN
Junior Colorist, June 2001-October 2001, August 1997-September 1998
Assisted colorist, Applied hair color, Answered telephones, Booked appointments, and took cash.

WORM BOOKS, Albrecht, NY
Bookseller, November 2000-February 2001
Cashier, Music Sales, Filled special orders, Managed stock and inventory

Internship
HEAVY MUSIC MANAGEMENT
Intern, Summer 2002
Phones, Tracking Record Sales, Creating Flyers, Tracking
Publicity/Creating
Press Kits, Faxing, Copying, General Intern Activities.

Skills/Activities Only include relevant activities
-DJ and Gothic Programming Director for WFTU, the college radio station
-Active member of FTU Marketing Club
-Knowledge of word processing and personal computers.
Microsoft Works, Excel, Windows
-Knowledge of HTML, web page design language
-Licensed Cosmetologist in the state of New Jersey
-Big Red Records Focus Group

References Available Upon Request

LOOK HOW CLEAN AND TARGETED JORDAN'S RESUME BECOMES.

JORDAN HOPPER
2114 Muse Road, Ixnay, NY 07701
(732) 555-1352
Joho33@aol.com

Objective: An entry-level position in music marketing.

EDUCATION

RUNWAY UNIVERSITY, Purchase, NY
B.S. Degree, Merchandising Management, December 2003
GPA: 3.5. Presidential Scholar.

EMPLOYMENT

GORILLA MUSIC, Purchase, NY
Assistant Manager, November 2002 - Present
Gorilla Music is a cutting-edge polka fusion record label. As an assistant manager at Gorilla, I:

- Train and supervise employees
- Prepare orders for domestic and international customers
- Monitor inventory
- Create visual marketing displays
- Study Polish and Esperanto to better communicate with Eastern European customers

HEAVY MUSIC MANAGEMENT, Chicago, IL
Intern, May-August 2002
Heavy Music runs a very competitive internship program. Out of 120 applicants, two interns were selected. As a Heavy intern, I:

- Tracked record sales
- Created advertising flyers
- Compiled press kits
- Answered inquiries from clients and customers on phone

SWISH FABRICS
Assistant Manager, October 2000-October 2002
Swish is a premier vendor of designer fabric remnants. Responsibilities as an assistant manager included:

- Prepared fabric displays
- Handled bank deposits and opening funds
- Monitored floor sales

SKILLS AND ACTIVITIES
- DJ and Gothic Programming Director for WFTU, the college radio station
- Active member of FTU Marketing Club
- Knowledge of HTML, web page design language, Windows, Excel
- Proficient in Esperanto and Polish

VICTOR'S RESUME IS RAMBLING, AND NOT TARGETED TO HIS OBJECTIVE: AN ENTRY-LEVEL JOB AS A PRODUCTION ASSISTANT

Victor de la Cruz
2243 Martyr Rd.
Siempres, CA 92011
619 444-9257

Objective
To obtain a position in telemedia as a specialist and production assistant, where my knowledge in Telemedia Communication will be of value.

Education

Major: Media Communication Years Attended (1999-2003)
Trevose College, Canon College Cornucopia/Siempres, CA

GPA of 3.5, Phi Theta Kappa Society, Technical Design and Production Assistant

Applied practical assignments using the fundamentals of set design, theory and practice of construction, painting, basic lighting for stage in the college production of "Tommy", Trevose College (August 21, 2002-November 23, 2002).

Associate Of Science Degree, Management Years Attended (1983-1985)
Aubern Hills Community College Williamston, Michigan

GPA of 3.3, Michigan Office Workers of Michigan

Experience

Concept Operator, Secretary Years Employed (1992-1999)
The Protectors Insurance Company San Diego, California

Maintained word processing reports and updated LOTUS spreadsheet.
Performed various clerical tasks as Secretary/Receptionist for Patient Advocate/Case Management Departments. Duties also included typing reports, correspondence, memos, and answering telephones. Received a Granta Award 1990. Group Specialist (July 29, 1989 - July 26, 1991), assisted sales staff in servicing existing and new accounts for the marketing/sales department.

Clerk Typist Years Employed (1987-1992)
Time Temporaries San Diego, California

Temporary in Conservative Department typing correspondence and various documents for insultation contractors at SDG&E.

Clerk Typist Years Employed (1985-1986)
Department of Human Resources St. Paul, Minnesota

(Section of Fisheries)

Typed scientific and technical reports for fisheries staff, also maintained fishery files, and reports.

Skills

*Type 50 wpm.
*Proficient with Microsoft Windows 2000 and Windows XP
*Displaywrite III/IV programs for IBM PC, and Database/Lotus Notes 6 for IBM
*Graphic Design for MacIntosh, Adobe Photoshop, Adobe Illustrator, Pagemaker, and QuarkExpress.

VICTOR'S RIGHT ON TARGET NOW

Victor de la Cruz
2243 Martyr Rd.
Siempres, CA 92011
619 444-9257

OBJECTIVE
An entry-level production position in broadcast television.

EDUCATION

B.A. in Media Communication 2003
Saint Theodore College, Siempres, CA
GPA: 3.5, Phi Theta Kappa Society

REVELANT COURSEWORK
"Television Set Design" Grade Earned: 4.00
"Art Direction for Television and Film" Grade Earned: 4.00
"Television and Film Lighting: Theory and Applications" Grade Earned: 4.00
"Television Production" Grade Earned: 4.00
"Drama Direction" Grade Earned: 4.00

EXPERIENCE

Technical Design and Production Assistant 2002
- "Tommy," Thespiatic Players, Trevose College Theater
- Applied practical assignments using the fundamentals of set design and theory
- Assisted set construction, including carpentry, fabric preparation and set painting
- Arranging and maintaining stage lighting

Concept Operator, Secretary 1992-1999
- The Protectors Insurance Company, San Diego, California
- Maintained word processing reports and updated LOTUS spreadsheet.
- Performed various clerical tasks as Secretary/Receptionist
- Typed reports, correspondence, memos, and answering telephones
- Received a Granta Award for Multitasking Excellence 1990

SKILLS

- Type 50 wpm.
- Proficient with Microsoft Windows 95, MS Word, Corel WordPerfect 7
- WordPerfect6.1, WordPerfect 5.1
- Displaywrite III/IV programs for IBM PC, and Database/LOTUS 1-2-3 for IBM
- Graphic Design for MacIntosh, SuperPaint, Adobe Photoshop, Adobe Illustrator, Pagemaker, and QuarkExpress.

LOOK AT HOW CRAMPED AND CONFUSED THIS RESUME IS! THE "SUMMARY" IS BOTH RAMBLING AND UNNECESSARY. AND DOES ANYONE CARE ABOUT POPPY'S READING MATERIAL?

Poppy Lorimer
4492 Mush Road
Anchorage, AK 99922
(907) 281-0758

SUMMARY
Creative individual uniquely qualified with expertise in the following areas: human resource systems, management and supervision, training and education, leadership initiatives, public relations and marketing. Thorough understanding of the strategic importance of human resources in the overall business context. Keen awareness and sensitivity to developing a competitive advantage through recruiting and managing a highly skilled, motivated, and services based workforce. Excellent written and verbal communication skills.

EDUCATION & TRAINING
Master's degree in organizational management - University of Alaska, Anchorage, AK
B.S. degree in human resources management - University of Alaska, Anchorage, AK
A.A. degree, major in psychology - Frontier State College, Palmer, AK
Mediation and Counseling for HR Practitioners, Nashville TN
1st year- Institutes for Organizational Management, University of Washington, Seattle, WA
Excellence in Leadership: Managing for Impasse - San Mateo, CA
Targeted Selection interviewing - DDI - Atlanta, GA

WORK EXPERIENCE
Operations Manager, Human Resources (exempt level) 2002-present
TBM,-Anchorage, AK
Human resources consultant partnering with 30+ first- and second-line managers in a multi-site client group environment, including multiple business segments, with strong emphasis in customer service. Areas of expertise: compensation analysis, behavioral interviewing, exempt level recruitment of technology positions through multiple avenues, performance appraisals, conflict resolution, leadership skills, employee relations, communicating organizational change succession planning, managing a remote and dedicated workforce, management training, contractor employment training, teamwork, coaching and counseling. Client population: 450-700, situated throughout the eastern one-half of the U.S., notably southeastern, northeastern, east coast states. (employment population: 6,500)
Client groups: network services, warehouse services and distribution, project management, and finance.
Training received: behavioral interviewing, leadership skills, management, sexual harassment

Office Administrator/ Manager (exempt level position)
2001-2002
DCM, Inc.
DCM, Inc. is a high quality manufacturing facility.
Management of office staff, accounting systems, financial reconciliation

Developed HR system; procedures, interviewing, screening, file maintenance, policies and procedures manual, coaching and counseling, conflict resolution
Reorganized office systems and procedures providing greater efficiency
Maintained information systems software and hardware
Developed strategic staffing projections for plant expansion
Developed pro forma statements and financial plans for plant expansion

Employee Relations Specialist (exempt level position)
1998-2001
Pontiac Regional Health Systems, Inc.
Managed employee retention and recognition programs, initiatives, events and activities
Organized and facilitated new employee orientation
Resolved employee relations issues
Back up for benefits specialist and HR generalist
Produce continuing media presentation to all employees:
Pontiac News
Network
Produced medical center newsletter
Assisted VP of Human Resources and CEO with special projects
Department IT Representative
Formerly Public Relations & Communications Specialist
Client population: 700+

Director, Programs & Services (exempt level, former Acting Executive Director) 1993-1998
Chamber of Commerce, Gallatin, TN
Fiscal responsibility, accounting systems management
Managed and supervised organization programs, membership, staff
Successfully recruited staff, businesses and industries, members
Effectively conducted seminars and workshops: small business startup and consulting
Public relations and marketing on behalf of organization and community
Public speaking on behalf of the chamber of commerce and community
Coordinated special events for community, non-profit fundraising
Converted all organizational systems and activities to computerization
Membership population: 475+

SOFTWARE KNOWLEDGE
Fully conversant with all Microsoft and Lotus product, and publishing software.

LOOK HOW MUCH BETTER AND READABLE POPPY'S RESUME IS NOW!

Poppy Lorimer
4492 Mush Road
Anchorage, AK 99922
(907) 281-0758

EDUCATION & TRAINING

M.A. in Organizational Management
B.S. in Human Resources Management
University of Alaska, Anchorage, AK

WORK EXPERIENCE

Operations Manager, Human Resources Department *2002-present*
TBM, Anchorage, AK

- Partnering with 30+ first- and second-line managers in a multi-site client group environment, including multiple business segments, with strong emphasis in customer service
- Providing compensation analysis, behavioral interviewing, for exempt level recruitment of technology positions
- Conducting performance appraisals, conflict resolution, management and leadership training for an employment population of over 6,500

Office Administrator/Manager *2001-2002*
DCM, Inc., Anchorage, AK

- Management of office staff, accounting systems, financial reconciliation
- Developed HR systems and procedures, including:, interviewing, screening, conflict resolutions, file maintenance techniques
- Created DCM's first policies and procedures manual, a guide to coaching and counseling
- Maintained information systems software and hardware
- Developed strategic staffing projections for plant expansion
- Developed pro forma statements and financial plans for plant expansion

Employee Relations Specialist *1997-2001*
Pontiac Regional Health Systems, Inc., Anchorage, AK

- Managed employee retention and recognition programs, initiatives, events and activities
- Organized and facilitated new employee orientation
- Resolved employee relations issues
- Produced continuing media presentation to all employees

Director of Programs & Services *1992-1997*
Chamber of Commerce, Gallatin, TN

- Fiscal responsibility, accounting systems management
- Managed and supervised organization programs, membership, staff
- Successfully recruited staff, businesses and industries, members
- Coordinated special events for community, non-profit fundraising

SOFTWARE KNOWLEDGE
Microsoft Windows, MS Word, Lotus Notes 6, Quark Express

About the Authors

Howard Leifman

Howard Leifman (Ph.D., New York University) has over 20 years of experience in human resources, staffing & recruiting, and career counseling as a principal and the National Director for Strategic Staffing and Recruiting for William M. Mercer, Inc., and a Senior Consultant in recruiting, training, and development at Towers Perrin. He has counseled and coached over 4,000 MBA students at the NYU Stern Graduate School of Business.

Marcy Lerner

Marcy Lerner lives in New York and is the Executive Editor at Vault. She holds an MA in history from Yale University.